Scriptures are taken from the King James Version and the New King James Version of the Holy Bible.

Plow On Publications
A division of Paul E. Tsika Ministries, Inc.
Restoration Ranch
5351 Hwy. 71
Midfield, TX 77458

www.plowon.org

Library of Congress Cataloging-In-Publication Data

Printed in the United States of America

DEDICATION

For me, dedicating a book is like trying to fit the missing piece of a jig saw puzzle. You want the one that fits.

This dedication is a perfect fit for "Releasing Your Full Potential."

I'd like to dedicate this book to my three sons:
Paul Edward Tsika II
Thomas James Tsika and
Mark Alan Rush (my daughter's husband)

These three men demonstrate in their marriages, relationships and personal lives, the principles in this book.

I am so proud of the ownership they have each taken over their life. As a father, I could not have asked for more. After college, they began the adventure of finding their place, and they have been willing to do whatever it takes in that pursuit. In this season of their life, they have found that place. But they know that life is a journey with twists and turns, and seasons can be long or short. While they are content, they are still learning, growing and changing to prepare for the next season.

Mark is the Executive Director at Paul E. Tsika Ministries, INC (Restoration Ranch). He oversees ranch operations and spends much of his time on the phone or in person counseling with couples. He has a Master's Degree from Southwestern Baptist Theological Seminary. Before beginning his service at the Ranch in 2015, Mark was involved in local church ministry, serving churches in Texas and California for 25 years. Most recently he served as Executive Pastor of Immanuel Baptist Church, Highland, CA.

Paul serves as the Lead Pastor of Grace Community Fellowship West Houston in Katy, Texas. Paul has been in full time Christian ministry for 27 years during which he earned his Master's degree from Southwestern Baptist Theological Seminary. He pastored in North Texas for 6 years and served as Executive Director of Paul E. Tsika Ministries, INC (Restoration Ranch) for 12 years. Paul ministers in local and foreign mission outreaches and preaches conferences for churches across the nation. Paul's top three passions are faith, family and friendships.

Thom is the CFO of Paul E. Tsika Ministries, INC (Restoration Ranch). He oversees all administrative and financial responsibilities of the ministry. In addition to that, he serves as a personal assistant and financial advisor to Billie Kaye and Me. He attended and played golf for Oklahoma City University and Mars Hill University. After graduation Thom worked as the Junior Head Golf Professional at Mountain Air CC, while also serving as the head golf coach at Mars Hill University, Mars Hill, NC. After playing 3 years on the mini tours, he joined Paul E Tsika Ministries full time.

These three men, now married 29, 28, and 25 years, bless, inspire, encourage and challenge me to want to be a better man.

And so, THANK YOU my sons, for loving me and helping me to end well.

-Dad

ACKNOWLEDGMENTS

Most of all, I want to acknowledge all those who have a hunger to experience God's best for their life. You know who you are, and you're many. I pray this book with empower you even more to achieve that most worthy goal. Your relentless pursuit to give your utmost for God is all inspiring. Thank you.

Rey Reynoso. *For his efforts in laying out "Releasing" in an easy to read format. He also did the layout for "Dining With The Diamonds" that Billie Kaye compiled. Web address: www.reyreynoso.com*

Dr. J. Tod Zeiger. *We have ministered together many times through the years. His teachings and insights have made a great contribution to my life and the contents of this book.*

Mercury Press, Oklahoma City. *For almost 20 years they have helped with the printing of my books. Gary and Cheryl Wright own Mercury Press and have been dear friends through thick and thin. Jim Howlet is our hands on connection at Mercury and a great blessing.*

Wayne Kerr. *This talented young man does all our cover designs. Both for our DVD sets and now this book. We love the way he thinks and is able to make our ideas become reality. Web address: www.waynekerrmusic.com*

Billie Kaye Tsika. *She tells me she can find errors in the best of books. Well she has found no less than 500,000 in "Releasing." I really appreciate her tireless effort in proofing the text, over and over and over and over again. Love you hon.*

CHAPTER 1 1
ATTITUDE DETERMINES ALTITUDE
The Missing Ingredient of Successful Leadership

CHAPTER 2 21
THE JOSEPH PRINCIPLE
The Anatomy of A Successful Leader

CHAPTER 3 37
WHY LEADER'S FAIL...
But You Don't Have To!

CHAPTER 4 57
BEWARE OF THE VISION STEALERS
They Are Everywhere

CHAPTER 5 71
MAPPING YOUR DESTINY
Your Roadmap To Success

CHAPTER 6 87
CLIMBING HIGHER
The View is Incredible

CHAPTER 7 109
A LIFE OF INTEGRITY
An Inside Job

CHAPTER 8 121
DEALING WITH DESTINY'S DETOURS
Don't Fret — Redirect

CHAPTER 9 135
COPING WITH CRITICISM
Respond Don't React

CHAPTER 10 155
THE PAST IS PAST
It's Time To Run!

CHAPTER 11 173
FINDING YOUR PURPOSE
Everyone Has One

CHAPTER 12 183
WHEN THAT WHICH YOU LOVE HAS DIED
Time To Raise The Dead

CHAPTER 13 197
DAILY CONFESSION
Release Your Full Potential Daily

CHAPTER 1

Attitude Determines Altitude
The Missing Ingredient of Successful Leadership

Kenny Rogers and the First Edition sang, in the 1960s, "I just dropped in to see what condition my condition was in."

Not a bad idea! It's probably time to allow the Holy Spirit to "drop in" and give us, as leaders, an attitude check. There are many talented, anointed leaders with such bad attitudes that no one wants to hear what they have to say, much less follow where they're going.

> **Proper Attitude + Anointing = Success**
> *But...*
> **Bad Attitude + Anointing = Failure!**

The word *attitude* is often used, and yet it's hard to explain, like *love* or *grace*. Says Maxwell:

> "Hardly a day passes without the word
> 'attitude' entering a conversation. It may
> be used as a complaint or a compliment.
> It could mean the difference between a
> promotion or a demotion. Sometimes
> we sense it, other times we see it, yet it is
> difficult to explain." (John Maxwell, *The
> Winning Attitude*)

Attitude is an inward feeling expressed by outward behavior. Or to put it another way, our actions are determined by our attitudes. And our attitude determines our altitude in Life. How high we go in our goals. Whether at church or in a normal business day, you will meet someone's attitude before you meet them!

A friend of mine tells of his teenage son's love for screeching volume from his car radio. "I always know when Jimmy's coming," says my friend, "because his radio arrives first, and he's not far behind."

Whether we like it or not, we are broadcasting attitudes all the time and they "arrive" before we do. We put out signals that tell people, "Don't mess with me ... I'm having a bad attitude day." What kind of attitude good or bad? *Attitude is the missing ingredient for successful leadership.*

Meet the elder brother in Luke 15: He's the poster boy for bad attitudes!

Let's allow the elder brother to help us with a four-step process to build a *bad* attitude.

■ **Step One:** *Get angry over something that you can't control or has nothing to do with you.*

The elder brother "was angry and would not go in" to the celebration his dad was giving for the younger son. Why? Things were happening over which he had no control. He heard music and dancing. A party was taking place, and he didn't like it one bit! Why is it, when we are in the middle of a pity-party, we can't stand for anyone else to be happy?

No one can make you angry. All others can do is reveal that you are angry already. It's the "pressure" principle. Whatever is inside will come out when there is sufficient pressure applied. If you squeeze a tube of glue you're not going to get toothpaste. The elder brother was already angry, the pressure of new circumstances revealed what was inside and it wasn't pretty when it came out.

■ **Step Two:** *Let your anger drive you to isolation.*

Luke 15:28 tells us the elder brother "would not go in." Anger is the root of bad attitudes. The one thing an angry person does not want is to go to a party (a place where people are happy and secure). They don't want to hear all the reasons they should join in. As a matter of fact, they have convinced themselves that it's best to "suffer in silence" and not trouble anyone else.

■ **Step Three:** *Get self-centered and stay there.*

Jesus describes how the older brother moans that he had never been given the favor shown his bratty, younger brother. "You never killed a goat for me," says the older. Says he:

> *"... Lo, these many years do I serve thee, neither transgressed I at any time thy commandment: and yet thou never gave me a kid, that I might make merry with my friends: But as soon as this thy son was come, which hath devoured thy living with harlots, thou hast killed for him the fatted calf."* (Luke 15:28-30)

Notice the use of *I*. At least five times he uses the personal pronouns *I* and *me*. He was more concerned about his rights than the fact that his brother had gotten out of the pig pen and returned to his father's house. His main concern: "Hey, what about me?" See what his anger and bitterness did? He got way out of focus. His vision of what was really important was obscured. He couldn't tell the difference between goat meat and baby beef (verses 28 and 29.) Talk about a bad attitude! Here it is in all it's glory (or should I say "gory"). Bitterness and unforgiveness will cause you to settle for goat meat while others are enjoying prime U.S.D.A ribeyes.

■   **Step Four:** *Jump in the pool of Self-Pity.*

Start by accusing someone else for your condition. The indignant brother tells his father, "... But as soon as this son of yours came..."(Verse 30). Notice, it's not "My brother" but "Your son." We want to blame someone else for what we're feeling and how we're acting; It's our wife, our boss, our pastor, our children, our up line or our down line. Anybody will do, as long as I don't have to *look in the mirror!*

Some Startling Facts about Attitude:

1.   YOU CAN CHOOSE YOUR OWN ATTITUDE.

The attitude you have today is the one you have chosen. Think about the last time you went to a major function. When you got to the door, were you greeted by a platinum who said, "Glad to see you this morning! My job is to hand out attitudes. Let's see, I have already given out too many positive ones, so you will have to have a negative one this morning." Maybe that sounds silly, something that could never happen. The way people act, however, not only on Sunday but also in the workplace, you would think someone *made* them have a bad attitude.

In my marriage seminars, I like to get feedback, so I start each session by asking what was learned in the last one. Without exception, the response is, "Attitude is a choice." It seems a light goes on, and they realize that they *are* in control of their own attitudes. I heard someone say, "God chooses what we go through, but we choose how we go through it." Some people get better while others get bitter. Some are sad while others are glad. It's all a matter of choice!

One Sunday morning, at a large church in Alabama, a woman visitor encountered the toughest-looking man she had ever seen. In a later time he might have been type-cast as Godzilla. A natural snarl was carved into his face. His utterly bald head shone starkly in the Sunday morning light. The woman tensed as he approached her. He extended a bulletin to her and suddenly the breaker of a big smile washed up on what had seemed the foreboding, gritty beach of his face.

Later, the woman wrote a note to the church's pastor:

> "I had awakened this morning with
> the intention of killing myself today. I
> promised the Lord I would go to church,
> and if Jesus somehow reached out to me, I
> would change my mind. That usher's smile
> was the touch of Jesus for me and saved my
> life."

The usher himself could have chosen bitterness over the way he looked. He could have had a bad attitude, because in a church full of white-collar executives, he was a "common laborer." He might have reasoned that since God seemed to have created him with a natural grimace, he didn't have to smile.

But the usher made an attitudinal choice and a human being was saved.

2. THE DIRECTION OF YOUR LIFE WILL BE DETERMINED BY YOUR ATTITUDE.

William James was wrong in some areas, but not when he said, "the greatest discovery of my generation is that people can alter their lives by altering the attitudes of their mind."

Actually, William James was late in making that "discovery." Centuries earlier the Holy Spirit had revealed that, "as he thinks in his heart, so is he" (Proverbs 23:7). If you expect failure and are always speaking with a negative tone, guess what you're going to get? I'm amazed at the number of people who don't have a clue where they are going, and they wonder why their attitude is so bad.

Years ago, as a first grader, a friend of mine was running through the school playground during recess. It was the late 1940s, and his mother had dressed him in knickers. The kid was wondering why his mother wanted to torture him by forcing him to wear pants that gathered above his ankles and puffed out like two oblong balloons up to his waist.

Just then, as he scampered with all the speed a first grader could muster, he ran into a huge, tin bucket left in the schoolyard. Thankfully, the bucket was filled with rancid water and not paint. But as the child's feet collided with the bucket, the water splashed out onto his loathed knickers, the only good result of the whole affair. Any one in his circumference got a dousing as well.

But my friend learned an unforgettable lesson: *Whatever fills your bucket is what will splash out on yourself and others.* It is inevitable that the "bucket" of our lives is going to get kicked. People are going to collide with us. What is inside is what will come out when they do. If it's a bad attitude, it's rancid bitterness will spill all around us. "Nothing can stop the man with the right mental attitude from achieving his goal," said W.W. Ziege, but "nothing on earth can help the man with the wrong mental attitude."

Our attitude determines what we can expect from life. Pointing ourselves in the right direction with the right attitude does not affect the world around us as much as it affects us. The first person soaked with the bad water when he "kicked the bucket" was my friend himself. We cannot expect change to come from outside - it has to start *within* us!

Theron Stallworth, a 23-year old Knoxville school teacher, was determined to help his inner-city students learn this vital lesson. As he laid on assignments, his sophomores would lament, "we can't do this."

So Stallworth decided to have a funeral for "can't." At first, the pupils thought it a joke. But one Thursday, they found they were attending a "funeral," complete with mourners, flowers and a white casket.

The students wondered what was inside the casket containing the corpse of "can't." Would it be a doll, a picture? As the high-schoolers peered into the casket, they were shocked, individually, to see their own image. Stallworth had lain a mirror in the box. As the students gazed in to look upon the deceased "can't" they were looking at themselves!

Knoxville *News-Sentinel* reporter David Keim recorded excerpts from Stallworth's "eulogy":

> "I want you to know there is a world out
> there waiting for you to overtake it," he
> preached. He urged the girls to live with
> integrity, and the boys to be leaders. "Any
> guy can be a father, but it takes a real man
> to be a dad," he said, to applause from the
> girls. "We have lawyers in here, and we
> have doctors in here, and we have world

class entrepreneurs here. In here, folks! We
are going to break the stigma that exists at
this school!"

It was the first time many of the students understood that attitude
is a choice.

3. **THERE IS A THIN LINE BETWEEN SUCCESS AND FAILURE.**
That little line is sketched in one word - *attitude*!

When Israel arrived at the borders of the promise land, we
would expect a stampede to get in and possess it. Instead, they did
the safe thing. They sent spies to check it out and see if it was true - as
if God would lie to them! When the spies returned, instead of praise
and joy we hear unbelief and doubt. As I was reading the account, I
was struck by the difference between the ten who said, "We are not
able to go up against the people, for they are stronger than we," and
Caleb and Joshua who said, "Let us go up at once and take possession,
for we are well able to overcome it."

In those two contrasting attitudes, we see the differences between
winners and losers. Let's look more closely at the distinguishing
characteristics between the two attitudes.

> **Losers are always looking at the obstacles**
> **Winners look at obstacles as opportunities**
>
> **Losers ask, "Why?"**
> **Winners ask, "Why not?"**
>
> **Losers are stopped by fear**
> **Winners are energized by results**
>
> **Losers make excuses**
> **Winners never need them**
>
> **Losers are easily discouraged**
> **Winners never stop, they possess the spirit of a bulldog!**

THREE GREAT BIBLE ATTITUDES

The Attitude of Jesus.

We would expect history's greatest leader to have the greatest attitude. Paul said, "Let this mind (attitude) be in you that was also in Christ Jesus." All we have to do is watch his actions, listen to His words, and we know that He was the master of His own attitude. Hebrews 12:2 says we are to "look unto Jesus, the author and finisher of our faith, who for the joy set before Him endured the cross, despising the shame, and has sat down at the right hand of the throne of God."

Here are three key facets of Jesus' winning attitude:

■ **Jesus knew why He was here.**

He wasn't *confused* about His *purpose.* Jesus was very sure as to why He was here, what He was to do, and who sent Him! If we believe we are here for a purpose, we will live in the present moment of divine destiny. We will not wander, be confused, or live with negativity or doubt. The enemy tries to convince us that we are the only person ever born without purpose. It's a lie. Call it a lie. Believe it's a lie. Then, start to live like it's a lie! God has a purpose for every life.

■ **Jesus knew what He was sent to do.**

He was *clear* about His *mission.* Knowing we have a purpose is only the first step in defining that purpose. There has to be a "why" attached to it. Again, Jesus is very clear. Look at Jesus' "I am come" statements:

> " . . . to fulfill the law" (Matthew 5:17)
> " . . . to bring a sword" (Matthew 10:34)
> " . . . to send fire on the earth" (Luke 12:49)
> " . . . to give sight to the blind" (John 9:39)

> **" . . . to bring light to the world" (John 12:46)**
> **" . . . to seek and save the lost" (Luke 19:10)**

Jesus defined His mission statement, even without the proliferation of "how-to" books today: *"I am come that they might have life, and have it more abundantly."* John 10:10

■ **Jesus knew where He was going.**

He was *sure* of His *destiny.* The one thing the enemy hated about Jesus was the fact that He knew His destiny. The Devil tried to do all he could to stop Him. Jesus' experience in the wilderness was about Satan's attempts to detour His destiny!

Jesus expressed His destiny in the "I go" statements:

-*" . . . and then I go unto him that sent me."* **(John 7:33)**
-*" . . . for I know whence I came, and where I go."* **(John 8:44)**
-*" I go to prepare a place for you."* **(John 14:2-3)**
-*" I must needs go through Samaria."* **(John 4:4)**

No wonder Jesus had such a great attitude! No wonder the enemy wants to kill *your* attitude. When we look at the life of Jesus we can see why there was so much pressure on Him. Men and women who know their purpose, mission and destiny cannot be stopped!

The Attitude of Paul

The book of Philippians is Paul's declaration of joy written from prison. In it he gives us a four-fold secret of success for building a great attitude. If the Elder Brother is the poster-boy for bad attitudes, then Paul is the example for great attitudes! In the book of Philippians, we see how Paul captures the "attitude thieves." Let's identify the four thieves and Paul's four weapons:

■ **Capture the Thief of "Difficult Circumstances" with the attitude of a** *focused* **mind.**

> *"For to me to live is Christ, and to die is gain."* (Philippians 1:21)

In chapter one, Paul outlines his difficult circumstances but does not allow them to rob him of his joy. Though he is in prison, and he is certainly not living to enjoy his circumstances, it is clear that he is living to serve Christ. That's the focused mind!

Paul's present perspective was literally framed by the bars of a prison, and yet his gaze remained firmly fixed on his mission and purpose in Christ. Whatever your difficulty at present, the principle of focusing on the things of Jesus will cause them to shrink. Have you ever tried to focus on two things at once? Not only can't it be done, the attempt can cause tremendous headaches and even temporarily affect vision! *"Seek first the Kingdom of God, and His righteousness, and all these things will be added unto you."* (Matthew 6:33)

■ **Capture the Thief of "Other People" with the Attitude of a** *humble* **mind.**

> *"Let nothing be done through strife or vainglory; but in lowliness of mind let each esteem others better (more important) than themselves."* (Philippians 2:3)

In the first chapter of Philippians, Paul puts *Jesus* first, but in chapter two he puts *others* second. That means he views himself last! The reason *others* bothers us is that we all want our own way. When we demand our way, the pursuit of our own rights gets us into trouble.

Often we allow those around us, well meaning or not, to steal our joy through the infectiousness of their own negativity and poor attitudes. If joy is a disease, then let's all be carriers. Let's infect others instead of *being* infected.

■ **Paul captures the thief of "Worldly Things" with the attitude of the *Spirit-filled* mind.**

> *"They that are dominated or controlled by the flesh are so because they mind (fill their life with) the things of the flesh but those who are controlled by the Spirit are so because they mind (fill their life with) the things of the Spirit . .who set their mind on earthly things."*
> (Romans 8:5)

Eleven times in this chapter Paul uses the word "things." The spiritually minded Christian is concerned about heavenly things. The spiritually minded man looks at the things of this world with Heaven's point of view (v. 20). Strong words are used by Paul in this passage to describe the "enemies of the cross." He makes it very clear that these enemies are those things which appeal to our baser, fleshly appetites. They are enemies (opposites) of the Cross of Christ since the Cross is the very essence of sacrificing self for the love of the Father and of others. The spirit-led life is one which values calling over covetousness, and destiny over personal desire. Paul loved and served people and used things but never loved and served things and used people.

■ **Paul captures the Thief of "Worry" with the Attitude of the *guarded* mind.**

> *"Be anxious (worried) for nothing but in everything by prayer and supplications with*

thanksgiving let your request be made known to God." (Philippians 4:6)

Worry is wrong thinking (the mind) and wrong feeling (the heart) about difficult circumstances, other people, and worldly things. Worry is an attitude killer! I am amazed at the attitude of many believers when it comes to worry. "Why pray when you can worry?" This is the most prevalent attitude in the church. I'm reminded of the Christian brother who came to a fellow church member concerning a situation asking for agreement in prayer. "Has it come to that?" was the startled reply. For many in the church, prayer is reserved for the crisis situations of our personal and corporate lives. Otherwise, we essentially tell God, "Thanks anyway, but I'm rather enjoying my dilemma at the moment. When it gets to be too much, I'll yell!"

Paul describes the *guarded* mind this way: *"And the peace of God, which passes all understanding, shall keep (guard) your hearts and minds through Christ Jesus"* (Philippians 4:7). The word "keep" in this verse is the word used by the military of Paul's day to refer to the "watch" posted on three hour rotations throughout the night. At no time could the enemy catch them by surprise. The peace of God is an ever-vigilant soldier at the gate of our souls keeping worry from carrying out its covert mission.

The Attitude of David (Psalm 34)

Here is a man who had all kinds of trouble and pressure, and yet he learned the secret of a positive attitude - praise! Before it was ever scripture, as we know it in *Psalms,* he could say, *"Rejoice in the Lord, and again I say rejoice!"* Listen to the Heart of Positive Praise. David knew three important truths about the power of praise:

Praise is a decision:

"I will Bless The Lord at all times..." (Psalm 34:1)

Once again, it's a matter of choice. In most churches, we depend on the worship team to "get us going" on Sunday morning. What do you think would happen if we all came together and made a decision of our will that we praise God, no matter what kind of week we had or how badly we had been treated at home or on the job? I believe we would see unparalleled freedom in our worship and would experience the presence of God in an awesome way. Just like David, we can *choose* to praise Him! Same thing in life. No matter what our circumstances, we make a choice to rejoice and have an attitude of gratitude.

Praise touches the emotions.

"My soul shall make its boast in the Lord..." (Psalm 34:2)

David knew his emotions would lie to him. He knew the secret. He asked himself, *". . . soul why are you cast down?"* In other words, go ahead and praise Him and your emotions will catch up! Our spirit-man *should* rule, but for most of us our emotions are in control. Our mind, will and emotions dominate us. We should dominate them!

Praise is contagious:

"...the humble shall hear of it and be glad." (Psalm 34:2)

Speaking of the "new song" God put in his mouth, David proclaimed, *"Many shall see it, and turn . . ."*(Psalm 40:3).

Paul and Silas are great examples of positive praise in bad circumstances. They were beaten, put in prison and at midnight, instead of complaining, they were praising! Their praise led to an earthquake, a jail full of prisoners being released and the very man who put them there coming to Christ. The world is waiting and watching for a person who will praise God in the midnight hour.

The way to grow in the area of our attitude is to approach the changes that must be made the same way any gardener or farmer approaches growth. With the soil made fertile through the work of the Holy Spirit, we need to sow the seeds of a great attitude and allow God to grow them. Allow me to suggest five attitude seeds to plant. Remember, seeds become giant trees when they are allowed to grow!

Seed #1 <u>Don't live life looking in the rear-view mirror.</u>

Stop living in the past! Paul said it best: *"But one thing I do, forgetting those things which are behind . . ."* (Philippians 3:13). What would happen if we drove our cars always looking behind and never to the front? We could get ourselves killed! Too many people live their lives in the memory of past defeats. Paul had a terrible past, yet he lived his life knowing that the blood of Jesus Christ cleansed him from all past hurt, defeat and failure.

Seed #2 <u>Learn to hang around people who are going somewhere.</u>

I have a saying: *"If you're going to carry someone's briefcase, make sure they know where they are going!"* If you spend all of your time and energy with negative people, guess where you will end up? In the same ditch they are in! *"He who walks with wise men will be wise"* (Proverbs 13:19). Athletes trying to lift their game to the next level are always looking for someone to train with who is better than them. Think of those with whom you spend the greatest amount of your time. Are they going somewhere? Are they going in the direction you wish to go?

Seed #3 <u>Live to Rejoice in Today.</u>

This is the only day you have. Make the best of it. *"This is the day the Lord has made; We will rejoice and be glad in it"(Ps.118:24).* This adage puts it just about the best way it can be said: *"Yesterday is history. Tomorrow is a mystery. Today is a gift. That's why it's called the present!"* Far too many of us are "history buffs" when it comes to attitude. Whether we let the failures of the past convince us we can't succeed today or the successes of the past lure us into living them again and again, our past can obstruct our future. The only good reasons to remember the past are encouragement and instruction. If it was good, be encouraged that more good can happen. If it was bad, learn from it and don't do it again!

Seed #4 <u>Lighten Up</u>!

What a relief it is to know that the whole kingdom's advancement doesn't depend solely upon you! We need to learn that God has a wonderful sense of humor. (If you don't think so, go to the mall, sit down and watch for a while - or look in your mirror)! Stop taking yourself so seriously, learn to laugh and remember: It takes more muscles to frown than it does to smile. *"These things have I spoken unto you, that My joy may remain in you, and that your joy may be full"* (John 15:11). *"A merry heart makes a cheerful countenance, . . ."* (Proverbs 15:13).

Seed #5 <u>Learn to Love Change—It's here to Stay</u>.

Nothing produces fear like change. Another saying I have is, *"Blessed are the flexible, for they shall bend but not break."* It's hard to think about change when we are in our comfort zone, especially in business. God has a way of letting us get it all together and then walking in one day and rearranging everything. You might as well love it, because change is going to be around for a long time! (More on change in a later chapter.) *". . . but be transformed by the renewing of your mind"* (Romans 12:2). Remember, "methods are many but values are few, methods may change but values never do."

Now that we have seen the proper approach to building a bad attitude (the elder brother), looked at three great Bible attitudes (Jesus, Paul and David), and planted five attitude seeds, let's complete the process by examining five steps to building a great attitude:

1.   BELIEVE THAT GOD PUT YOU HERE FOR A PURPOSE.

You are not an accident! *"Before I formed you in the womb, I knew you. Before you were born I sanctified you; . . ."* (Jeremiah 1:5.) We need to get that word deep into our spirits. Some people live like they are the only ones who were put on this earth without a purpose, plan or destiny. Satan's great lie is that we don't matter in the Kingdom plan. If you have been listening to this lie to any extent, stop it! Believe the truth of the Word of God. You are uniquely created, called and commissioned to make a difference. It's time to get on with it, isn't it? Our mission statement in World Wide says that, "God created you for greatness." Never settle for less.

2.   STOP LOOKING FOR THE NEGATIVES.

There are things in our lives we didn't choose and really can't do anything about. For instance - our place of birth, our family, our upbringing, etc. As a matter of fact, even the face we look at in the mirror every day is not an option. We can't trade it in for a new one! There are, however, things we can do something about. Think about the people with which we spend the most time. If we're listening to negative people all the time, guess what is going to happen? We begin to sound and act just like them. If we choose to spend time with positive people, we will find ourselves becoming more positive. Anyone can identify the problems, but winners find solutions.

3. LOOK AT THE OPPORTUNITIES, NOT THE PROBLEMS.

The Apostle Paul is a great example of a man who overcame his problems and turned them into great opportunities. In Philippians chapter one, he details his difficulties. He focused his desire on the spread of the gospel not on potential problems. If we spend all our time and energy worrying about our problems, we will increase our chances of being overwhelmed by them. Paul knew his situation was filled with danger, but he concentrated on others. He sums up his attitude this way, *"What then?. . . . In this I rejoice, yes and will rejoice"*(Philippians 1:18). When viewed in the right perspective, problems can be a blessing and not a curse. Problems give us an opportunity to grow, expand and reach for new and exciting opportunities.

4. LEARN TO GIVE YOURSELF AWAY TO OTHERS.

Start today. Choose to invest in the lives of others. One of the best ways to bring a quick adjustment to my attitude is to get my eyes off myself and onto someone else who is struggling more than I am! We can never out-give God. The principle of Luke 6:38 is still true today: *"Give and it shall be given unto you."* Your rewards in life will always be in direct proportion to the problems you solve for others.

5. DON'T EVER QUIT!.

Stay the course! Life is littered with drop-outs. Anyone can quit. It takes a real man or a real women to stay in the fight and pursue destiny. Paul told Timothy, *". . . Make full proof of your ministry"*(2Timothy 4:5). In other words, don't shut up, don't back up and don't give up on your God-called purpose. I want it to be said of me, like Paul, *"He finished his course!"* With reckless abandon, I pursue with passion my purpose.

LET PEACE AND CONTENTMENT RULE YOUR LIFE.
Philippians 4:10-13

CHAPTER 2

The Joseph Principle
The Anatomy of A Successful Leader

The name Joseph means "increase" or "increaser." God's purpose and desire is for us to increase in our knowledge and skill. Joseph was on a journey of increase. Mark 4:23-25 gives us this wonderful principle. In short, it tells us that the more we want, the more we can have. If we don't use what we have been given we lose it. It's a pretty simple yet life-changing principle. In this chapter we will see how God increased the life of Joseph as He moved him through many stages in preparation for his ultimate destiny - the throne of Egypt.

JOSEPH — AN OLD TESTAMENT PICTURE OF A NEW TESTAMENT TRUTH

Much has been written about Joseph. In this study, we will discover that he is a wonderful "type" or illustration of the Lord Jesus, the ultimate overcomer.

As a type (Old Testament example) of Jesus:

- **He was the Beloved of the Father.**
  (Genesis 37:3)
- **He was sent on a Love Mission to His Brethren.**
  (Genesis.37:13)
- **He was sold for Pieces of Silver.**
  (Genesis 37:28)
- **He was Tempted - As we are, Yet without Sin.**
  (Genesis 39:7-12)

- **He Suffered for the Sins of Others.**
  (Genesis 39:20)
- **Man Placed Joseph in Prison, but the King brought him out.**
  (Genesis 41:14)
- **Joseph foretold the coming of the Great Tribulation.**
  (Genesis 41:29-30)
- **Joseph had a Gentile Bride. (Genesis 41:45)**

> **What We Are about to Discover Is This:**
> **Joseph Was on a Journey - So Are You!**

The inner heart of a real leader knows he is on a journey. There is a recognition of an innate calling and purpose . . . of being created for something specific and extraordinary. The sad truth is that most leaders don't have a clue what that calling is. They think that, because they have a position of leadership, they have arrived at their final destination. God wants us to know that there is more - much more! In the words of that great Philosopher, Yogi Berra: "If You don't know where you're going, you could wind up somewhere else."

The Children of Israel were on the most famous trip to nowhere of all time. They wandered in circles in the wilderness for forty years, never taking any ground and never reaching their destination. The average local church leader, as well, stays in a holding pattern, going in circles but getting nowhere. Like the children of Israel, never seeming to arrive at the desired place of leadership guarantees that frustration and disappointment are just around the corner. Success in leadership is a journey:

> "You don't suddenly become successful
> when you arrive at a particular place or
> achieve a certain goal. But that doesn't
> mean you should travel without identifying

a destination. You can't fulfill your purpose and grow toward your potential if you don't know what direction you should be going."

—*John Maxwell*

> **Remember, leadership growth doesn't happen all at once!**

May I give you a definition of success that did not originate with me, but which I have used now for a long time? I call it the three "D's" of success:

Discover Why You are Here,

Determine to Reach Your Maximum Potential and

Devote Your Life To Enrich others!

The sad truth is that many in ministry define success as:

A. *Big Buildings*

B. *Bigger Baptisms (than anyone else in town)*

C. *Biggest Budgets*

The same can happen in a business setting. Definitions change but the principles don't. Make your own application and you will prosper from the principles.

We judge each other with "How many do you have in church?," rather than a definition of success that will sustain us when it doesn't look like we have the "biggest" thing in town! Somehow I think God has a different view. In 1Corinthians 3:13, Paul tells us that every work will be "tried by fire" as to what "sort" it is, not what "size" it is. We use this scripture to talk about a future judgment, and that may be the case, but I am convinced that God loves starting "fires," not just in the future but <u>now</u> - present tense. He just walks in one day and sets the whole thing ablaze just to see what kind of building materials we have used! If it's "wood, hay and stubble" it will burn, but "gold, silver, and precious stones" will last, be purified, and glorify the King. Let's see the stages through which God took Joseph to reach his destination.

STAGE ONE — THE DREAM STAGE

Here was a young man with a dream. Look at Genesis 37 and see the two dreams God gave him.

> "Now Israel loved Joseph more than all his
> children, because he was the son of his old
> age. Also he made him a tunic of many
> colors. But when his brothers saw that
> their father loved him more than all his
> brothers, they hated him and could not speak
> peaceably to him. Now Joseph had a dream,
> and he told it to his brothers; and they hated
> him even more. So he said to them, 'Please
> hear this dream which I have dreamed: There
> we were, binding sheaves in the field.'"
> "'Then behold, my sheaf arose and also stood
> upright; and indeed your sheaves stood all
> around and bowed down to my sheaf.' And
> his brothers said to him, 'Shall you indeed
> reign over us? Or shall you indeed have
> dominion over us?' So they hated him even
> more for his dreams and for his words. Then
> he dreamed still another dream and told it to
> his brothers, and said, 'Look, I have dreamed
> another dream. And this time, the sun, the
> moon, and the eleven stars bowed down
> to me.' So he told it to his father and his
> brothers; and his father rebuked him and said

> to him, 'What is this dream that you have
> dreamed? Shall your mother and I and your
> brothers indeed come to bow down to the
> earth before you?' And his brothers envied
> him, but his father kept the matter in mind."
> (Genesis 37:3-11 NKJ)

There was nothing in his upbringing that would suggest a great future or outlook; the eleventh son and the twelfth child in his family, but that didn't stop him from having a dream. Prepare for it. Some will even hate you for being a dreamer (Gen.37:4-5!)

The first step in successful leadership is asking God for a dream. In other words, *Dare to Dream!* Human history is filled with men and women who dared to dream in the face of great opposition, adversity and persecution. But you won't have to invent or fabricate your dream, you will discover it as you walk by faith and obedience. God will make your purpose obvious. Just hang in there!

■   **Napoleon, despite humble parentage, became an emperor.**
■   **Beethoven brought to life his inner vision for music when he composed symphonies, even after he lost his hearing.**
■   **The great Greek orator Demosthenes stuttered! But he didn't stop talking!**

THE BIRTH OF A DREAM

Let's use marriage, the most intimate covenant between two people, to see how a dream is birthed: First the natural, then the spiritual (Corinthians.15:44-46).

Step One: Pursuit and Courtship (Christ pursued us!)

Preceding marriage, there is a time of intense courtship, right? No hour is too late and none too early to pursue the one you love. In the spirit, Christ pursued us and loved us so much that He wanted to bring us into His kingdom. There came a moment in time when we said "Yes, I will follow you!" Before a dream or vision can ever be birthed, there has to be an intense desire to have it, to know it, and to pursue it at all cost. I am convinced that no one has ever accomplished much in life, especially the life of the kingdom, without a dream. Step one, then, is to pursue at all cost. Do not be denied.

Step Two: Marriage (Two become one)

Lets look at the covenant ceremony. Standing before a pastor the lovers say vows, exchange rings, and life together begins. In the pursuit of a dream, there comes another moment when a real decision has to be made just as in a marriage ceremony. It's not just a pursuit, and it's not just words, but it's real commitment to destiny. It's an attitude that says, "I'm going for this no matter what it takes, no matter what it costs, and no matter what anyone says about it."

Step Three: Intimacy (Necessary for birth)

In the natural, the next item on the agenda is intimacy. Without it there will be no children born - none whatsoever! Paul talked about intimacy when he said, "That I may know Him." The word "know" is one of closeness or intimacy. What did Paul want to know? Three things: the power of His resurrection, the fellowship of His sufferings, and being conformed to His death. To know those things one would have to be very close to God: Feel His heart beat! Know His mind! When we get that close to Him, we don't have to wonder, "Does He have a dream for me?" I meet people regularly who wonder why they don't have a clue about vision and destiny. I start by asking them how much time they spend with Jesus. You see, for a baby to be born in the natural, the parents have to spend time together, right? In the spirit, for your dream to come alive, it is necessary to be so close to

Him that if He clears His throat, the response is, "Father, did you say something?"

Step Four: Conception (A seed finds a place)

When intimacy occurs, birth is not far behind. A seed finds it's place and life is imparted! In the spirit, every word of God has within itself the power to bring to pass the very thing that God intends. One of the main goals of my teaching is to impart enough seed that someone will go away pregnant! For seed to produce life, there has to be a fertile place for it to lodge. In the world of the farmer, he knows he can have the best seed in the world, but if the ground is not prepared, it will not produce a harvest. In other words, you don't walk out in the parking lot at church and sow seed and expect to come back and collect bushels of corn. It just doesn't work that way. Spend enough time with Him and I guarantee seeds will be dropping into your spirit. Before you know it you will be "as big as the side of a house" in the spirit!

Step Five: Gestation (A time of hidden development)

This is the time of hidden things. When a woman is pregnant there is a period of time before she starts "showing." As her time progresses, things start getting uncomfortable. Nothing tastes the same, shoes don't fit, and for unknown reasons, crying breaks out. Everything inside is changing, and some will tell you it's a very strange and weird time . . . .

The supernatural seed of God's dream drops into your spirit and suddenly things begin to change. It's an uncomfortable, strange, and sometimes weird experience for you, too. I find that many people give up on their dream at this stage. It becomes too hard and they are not willing to see it through to it's conclusion. Many want the success of leadership without any of the pain and sacrifice. We have been sold a bill of goods that says, if we experience any uncomfortable times, we must not be in God's will. Tell that to a pregnant woman. On second thought, don't! She will tell you in a heart beat that this is a necessary part of the birth process, and that without it, no baby will be born. Don't give up on your dream when it gets uncomfortable. It's going to get worse!

Step Six: Travail (An intense and painful process)

Labor pains (I'm told) can be some of the most intense pain a person can feel. You may be in this stage right now. Seed has found a place and you have been in the uncomfortable place of hidden development. Now is not the time to quit but to push on and let God complete the birth of your destiny. There are far too many "spiritual abortions." The intention of the enemy is to stop the baby (dream) from being born. He knows if he can stop it from coming forth, he can stop you.

> **Don't Give up on Your Dream When the Labor Pains Start. It's a Sign That Birth Is about to Happen!**

Step Seven: Birth! Listen to what Jesus said about it::

> *"A woman, when she is in labor, has sorrow,*
> *because her hour has come; but as soon as*
> *she has given birth to the child, she no longer*
> *remembers the anguish, for joy that a human*
> *being has been born into the world."*
> (John 16:21)

There is great joy in watching the birth of your dream, but there is more to come. After the dream stage we get to:

STAGE TWO — THE PROBLEM STAGE

Read the story of Joseph and you will not only be blessed, you will see yourself and understand stage two and three even better. (Genesis chapters 37-50)

Here was a man with a big dream—but bigger problems!

He was hated by his own family - even before he shared his dreams (Genesis 37:4). The blessing and favor of his father brought hatred from his brothers. At this point in his life, Joseph's dreams are at the most fragile, because they are so new. They are not established, and they don't have a track record. Sometimes those that are closest to us will be the ones attacking the most, since in the early stages, they are the ones who know us best. Some people are like "firefighters" - they will try to "put out" our dreams!!

When a seedling oak is only a year old, a child can tear it out by the roots. But once it's had some time to become firmly established, even the force of a hurricane can't knock it down.

1. **JOSEPH ENDS UP IN THE PIT!**
    What in the world is God up to?

Joseph is learning to develop a "Palace" mentality even when he is surrounded by the "pit" of bad circumstances. Guess what? You can, too! Notice in Genesis 37:23-36 how Joseph's brothers arrange for this wonderful Pit experience. **Watch the Progress:**

The Enemy Can't Take Away the Favor of Your Father!

Nobody likes the PIT! What if we imagine that PIT stands for **P**eople **I**n **T**raining! We may all agree that, although it isn't a pleasant place, lessons can be learned there:

The Pit is not Punishment. It's unrealistic to think that when our dreams are birthed there will be no more hard times; no pit experiences. The result of this kind of thinking is that we get down in the pit and start to feel sorry for ourselves thinking that God doesn't like us anymore, or somehow we've made Him angry. **Listen to what Jesus said:**

> *"Blessed are you when men hate you, and when they exclude you, and revile you, and cast out your name as evil, for the Son of Man's sake. Rejoice in that day and leap for joy! For indeed your reward is great in heaven, for in like manner their fathers did to the prophets."* (Luke 6:22-23)

> *"In this you greatly rejoice, though now for a little while, if need be, you have been grieved by various trials, that the genuineness of your faith, being much more precious than gold that perishes, though it is tested by fire, may be found to praise, honor, and glory at the revelation of Jesus Christ, whom having not seen you love. Though now you do not see Him, yet believing, you rejoice with joy inexpressible and full of glory."* (1Peter 1:6-8)

> *"And lest I should be exalted above measure by the abundance of the revelations, a thorn in the flesh was given to me, a messenger of Satan to buffet me, lest I be exalted above measure. Concerning this thing I pleaded*

with the Lord three times that it might depart from me. And He said to me, 'My grace is sufficient for you, for My strength is made perfect in weakness.' Therefore most gladly I will rather boast in my infirmities, that the power of Christ may rest upon me. Therefore I take pleasure in infirmities, in reproaches, in needs, in persecutions, in distresses, for Christ's sake. For when I am weak, then I am strong." (2 Cor 12:7-10)

*Paul knew (and we discover) that the power of God is released in the pit, and in our weakness, we find out where our true strength lies. It's in Him and not in us. Now watch:

"So it came to pass, when Joseph had come to his brothers, that they stripped Joseph of his tunic, the tunic of many colors that was on him. Then they took him and cast him into a pit. And the pit was empty; there was no water in it." (Genesis 37:23-24)

Look at the Pit from Joseph's point of view:

NO POWER (His coat of favor was taken away.)
NO PRESENCE (The pit was empty.)
NO PROVISION (No water.)

But, he didn't give up, give in, or roll over and die!

2. HE'S IN POTIPHAR'S HOUSE. IS THIS, THAT?
(GENESIS 39:1-20)

Is this the realization of his dream or just another stepping stone in the process of learning to rule? Many times we don't see what God is up to and miss out on His learning exercises. For Joseph, being in Potiphar's house would appear to start out well but end up badly. The final destination was at the right hand of Pharaoh.

I'm sure this was not the path Joseph would have chosen. If he thought it was tough in the pit, he hasn't seen anything yet! I'm sure he must have thought, "I have arrived at my destiny - I'm ruling and reigning, right?" Well, yes and no. Here comes one of the toughest tests leadership ever faces; the test of integrity. His character is being developed. At this point many will run. God places a very high priority on integrity and character. No matter what TV or the polls may say, integrity is leadership quality number one, without which all of us end up as failures.

The chronicles of history are filled with accounts of greatly gifted, zealous and vision-filled men and women who, for lack of this quality, came to quick and shameful ends. Ask King Saul about it. It took two years for the cracks in his character to be exposed, but when they were, there was a "bang" that was heard throughout the kingdom. Every time I talk to God about more power in my life, He talks to me about character. Without character we can't contain or control the power. The very thing we want will be that which will consume and destroy us. The saddest thing ever said about a leader was said of Saul: it was as though he were never anointed!

> *"O mountains of Gilboa, let there be no dew,*
> *nor rain upon you, nor fields of offerings. For*
> *the shield of the mighty is cast away there!*
> *The shield of Saul, not anointed with oil."*
> (2 Samuel 1:21)

Remember the apostle Paul: "You will appear before Kings." Wow! This is a great word, but he wasn't told how he would get there. (see Acts 26.)

For all of Joseph's trouble to protect his character, guess where he ends up?

3.   HE'S IN PRISON. THIS CAN'T BE THAT! (GENESIS 40)

God is getting him in position to fulfill his dream. Joseph is serving faithfully, Potiphar's wife tries to seduce him, and as he escapes with his life, she cries rape! From our point of view, what happened at Potiphar's house was a bad thing, but sometimes what we call bad, God calls good! Notice that Joseph didn't quit serving God, even in prison. Read Genesis 40, and see how God is getting the circumstances of Joseph's life ready for him to reach his destiny's fulfillment. He interprets two dreams (the butler and the baker, not the butcher and the baker) and says to them, "Remember me." Two years go by, and if you had talked to Joseph, he would have told you that maybe he missed it. Sometimes, we think God has forgotten where we live. If He could just remember our zip code! God didn't forget him, and He hasn't forgotten you. Keep serving where you are. Develop your potential and get ready, because the best is yet to come!

STAGE THREE — AT THE PALACE!

The fulfillment of the dream... Joseph is ruling, but how did he get here? We see the favor of God every step of the way. Over and over again in this account we see that God's hand was on him:

> "The LORD was with Joseph, and he was a successful man; and he was in the house of his master the Egyptian." (Genesis 39:2)

*"But the LORD was with Joseph and showed
him mercy, and He gave him favor in the
sight of the keeper of the prison."*
(Genesis 39:21)

*"And Pharaoh said to his servants, 'Can we
find such a one as this, a man in whom is the
Spirit of God?'"* (Genesis 41:38)

Successful leaders will have a "go-for-it" mentality. Look at
Joseph when the door opened to:

**Tell his dreams - in spite of opposition, he shared them.
For sin to short-circuit his dreams - he closed it.
To utilize his gifting - he walked through it, twice!
To let bitterness rule his heart over past hurt - he refused it!**

And the conclusion was this statement spoken to his brothers:

*"But as for you, you meant evil against me;
but God meant it for good, in order to bring
it about as it is this day, to save many people
alive."* (Genesis 50:20)

What was God really doing in preparing Joseph? God was
getting a man ready for a time in history. Read the dreams of Pharaoh:
Seven years of plenty followed by seven years of famine. God needed
a man to oversee both; a man of character, integrity, and discernment.
God knew what was coming and needed a Joseph to walk into the
courts of the king and say, "Here is what God says about it." When the
Pharaohs of this world begin to ask questions, God is going to have

men and women of character, integrity and discernment who can walk in and deliver the Word of the Lord. Much has been said about the Joshua Generation, the Caleb Company and others. I believe all of that is true, but let me tell you; God is raising up a people with a "Joseph Anointing" who will walk with an excellent spirit and literally astound the world with their wisdom and favor. When the world has questions, we will be ready with answers. No matter what "stage" we find ourselves in, or how we identify with Joseph, we must stay focused on our destiny. We must not let the enemy rob us of what God wants to do in our lives! We are destined for greatness, and by God's grace, no one and nothing will rob us of our destiny.

"The steeper the hill, the harder the climb. But the harder the climb, the greater the view from the top." —*Paul E. Tsika*

CHAPTER 3

Why Leader's Fail...
But You Don't Have To!

Leadership Rediscovered:

■ The key to success in our present circumstances is the ability to lead others successfully. Everything rises or falls on Leadership!

■ Our up-sets are set-ups from the enemy, who does not want us to reach our full potential. In most churches, we are put in places of leadership without a clue of what leadership is, how it works, or how we can become a successful leader. We have been set-up, so it's time to wake up!

■ Success is not just for a few: the select of the elect. If we possess desire, passion and a willingness to succeed, the characteristics of the raw materials of leadership can be acquired. We can learn, develop and hone the skills of leadership, even though we have been told that Great Leaders are born, not made.

Leonard Ravenhill, in the *Last Days Newsletter*, tells about tourists who were visiting a picturesque village. As they walked by an old man sitting beside a fence, one visitor asked in a patronizing way, *"Were any great men born in this village?"* The old man replied, *"Nope, only babies."*

Some may feel like babies right now in terms of leadership skills, but with the proper motivation, desire and training, the leadership skills that God intended can be acquired.

WHAT IS LEADERSHIP?

Books are written, seminars are held, and opinions abound, but very few people really understand leadership! How do I know? Walk the halls of the average church (yes, I know yours is not average) and ask ten people for a one line definition of leadership. Twelve different answers will be given!

J. Oswald Sanders in his book *Spiritual Leadership* said, *"Leadership is influence, the ability of one person to influence others."*

Leadership Is Influence - Period!

The greatest leadership proverb I have ever heard says, *"He who thinketh he leadeth and hath no one following is only taking a walk."* Whether we like it or not, we are influencing and being influenced by others. The awesome power of influence is being demonstrated in our lives every day. From birth until the day we die, influence is a major part of how we live and function.

James C. Georges, of the ParTraining Corporation says, *"Leadership is the ability to obtain followers."* If you don't have any followers, you are not leading. If you're talking and no one is listening, you're just exercising your own voice by talking to yourself.

Most people define leadership in terms of getting a position and not in terms of influencing followers. Hence, a gap appears. When we go after rank, title, or position, and get it, then we are leaders, right? *Wrong!* Here's the problem: When we pursue titles and the status of a leader, and no one is following, we get disappointed and the set-ups of the enemy are in place. At this point, we are ripe for the enemy's attack. Conversely, there are those who lack proper status, and may not see themselves as leaders, so they never bother to develop their leadership potential! In either case, disappointment is just around the corner.

Before We Go Any Further Consider This!

Before You Die, Whom Do You Want to Influence?

For What Do You Want to Be Remembered?

After You're Gone, What Do You Want People to Say About You?

What Do You Plan to Do With The Rest of Your Life?

Look at the story of the life of Dorcas as recorded in Acts 9:36-43. Verse 39 says "all the widows stood by him (Peter) weeping, showing the tunics and garments which Dorcas had made while she was with them." What an influence she was, even after she was gone!

On September 9, 1863, Confederate Lieutenant William R. McEntire was at the surrender of Cumberland Gap to Union forces. Years later, on his deathbed, he requested that his descendants return to the gap 100 years from the date of that surrender, stand at the pinnacle, and curse the Yankees for five minutes. His grandson did just that, on September 9, 1963 (Southern Living Magazine.) *That's influence — the wrong kind!*

The Dark Side of Leadership

There is an ancient Greek myth of Narcissus about a beautiful young man beloved of the nymphs. The nymph Echo fell in love with Narcissus's beauty, but he paid no attention to her. The gods looked upon unrequited love as a crime. So they punished Narcissus in appropriate symbolic form by causing him to fall in love with his own reflection, ever reaching out to embrace an illusion.

TEN CHARACTERISTICS OF A NARCISSISTIC LEADER

1. They have an inflated sense of importance, fantasies of unlimited fame, power and unquestioned adoration.
2. They have a deep need to be looked at and admired.
3. They feel rage with little justifiable cause.
4. They treat people with cool indifference as punishment when they are disagreed with.
5. They have a sense of superiority accompanied by the tendency to discredit and devalue people based on their inability to admit wrong.
6. While the Narcissist can get great results, it almost always ends in destruction, because of their inability to work with people they can't control.
7. Lying and deception are their means of elevating themselves.
8. They rule the emotional atmosphere everywhere they go, especially in the home.
9. They withdraw into grandiose fantasies to shield themselves from profound feelings of worthlessness.
10. Self love is learned through acceptance. Positive self regard is the opposite of what the narcissist experiences. He is in love with himself precisely because he cannot love himself.

HOW TO BE SET FREE

The main cause of this personality is insecurity. Security is a matter of trust. Fear is the opposite of faith which is trust. What frightens you?

Failing health — Growing old — Being alone — Being unimportant — Betrayal of friends — Unfaithful spouse — Being replaced — Being rejected — Loosing wealth & lifestyle — Looking stupid — Being disrespected — Failure — Loss of a loved one?

Nothing in this life comes more natural than fear. Fear is the opposite of faith and trust. When you run it out to the end and think about the worst thing that can happen to you, you'll find:

1. That all things work together for good to them that love God.
2. That what the enemy means for evil, God means for good.
3. All God's thoughts towards you are thoughts to bless you.
4. God's grace is sufficient.
5. That those that matter don't care and those that care don't matter.

> **Three Suggestions:**
> **Be honest with yourself.**
> **Be transparent with others.**
> **Be humble before God.**

Become the genuine/authentic follower and leader you were created to be. Value and respect others, honor God and live a life of NO REGRETS!!!

> **Always remember: God honors those who honor Him**
> **(1 Samuel 2:30)**

Twelve Traits Of Spiritual Leaders
(From Spiritual Leadership by J. Oswald Sanders)

1. **Spirit-filled:** Spiritual Leadership can be exercised only by Spirit-Filled men and women (Acts 6:3.)

2. Discipline: And they chose Stephen, a man full of the Holy Spirit (Acts 6:5.) This quality is placed first, for without it the other gifts, however great, will never realize their highest possibilities.

3. Vision: Those who have most powerfully and permanently influenced their generation have been the seers; men who have seen more and farther than others. Men of faith, for faith is vision.

4. Wisdom: Wisdom is the faculty of making the best use of knowledge, a combination of discernment, judgment, capacity and similar powers.

5. Decision: When all the facts are in, swift and clear decision is the mark of the true leader. The man of Vision must do something about it or he will remain a visionary, not a leader.

6. Courage: Courage of the highest order is demanded of a spiritual leader. Always moral courage and frequently physical courage as well.

7. Humility: In the realm of politics and commerce, humility is a quality neither coveted nor required. But in God's scale of values, humility stands very high. The spiritual leader of today is in all probability one who, yesterday, experienced humility by working gladly and faithfully in second place.

8. **Humor:**	Since man is in the image of God, his sense of humor is a gift of God and finds its counterpart in the divine nature.
9. **Patience:**	A liberal endowment of this quality is essential to sound leadership. Chrysostom called patience the queen of virtues.
10. **Friendship:**	It was said of Dr. A.B. Simpson, *"The crowning glory of his leadership was that he was a friend of man."*
11. **Tact:**	A ready appreciation of the proper thing to do or say.
12. **Reproduction:**	The responsibility of the spiritual leader is to reproduce and multiply himself. If he is to discharge his trust fully, he will devote his time to training young men to succeed, and perhaps even supersede him (II Timothy 2:2).

There are deep "ditches" on the leadership highway. Many who would lead stumble and fall into them. This is why leaders and would-be leaders fail. Example: I (like most people) don't like people who look down their nose at other people. But one day I found myself looking down my nose at those who look down their nose at others. There's a ditch on both sides of the road.

DITCHES TO AVOID ON THE LEADERSHIP HIGHWAY

■ **A wrong concept of Leadership**

People want to be led, inspired and challenged, not just managed. In the church, as well as in business, the old model of people management won't work any longer. Nowhere in scripture do we find admonitions from the Father to manage His people. In every case, in every type and in every model we are given, we see the role of the shepherd - the leader. God wants His leaders out front, speaking encouragingly, saying, "Come this way! Follow me." While managers are task oriented, God's leaders are goal and vision motivated and motivating. We should be able to say with the Apostle Paul, "Follow me, as I follow Christ!" People want to be shown what to do not just told what to do. "Do as I say, not as I do" will turn people off faster than a "B" movie.

Out of the personal growth of the leader, through a vital, genuine and empowering relationship with God, comes the fire with which His message is burned into the hearts of those who follow. It's simple: No fire - No followers. At least not for long. Wonder why large crowds aren't flocking to your message? Poke the coals a bit and check the fire in your heart. I've always said, "There's no action in the pew, because there's no unction in the pulpit."

■ **Undeveloped Growth Potential**

Walt Disney said, "It's what you learn after you know it all that counts." Jim Rohn believes that, "Formal education will make you a living, but self education will make you a fortune." Earl Nightengale proposed, "Study any one subject one hour a day and in five years you will be a leading authority in that field." Charles Tremendous Jones asserts, "Five years from now you will be the same person you are today except for two things: the books you read and the people with whom you associate." Ex Philadelphia Flyer, Bobby Clark, an all time NHL great, once said, "If you are always at your best, your best must be pretty mediocre." The Holy Spirit, speaking through Paul, admonishes, "Study to show yourself approved . . . ." Those who maintain a lifelong zest for learning are those who consistently remain at the top of their fields of endeavor. The attitude that says, "I put in my time in school; I know enough to get by" will produce a lifestyle of exactly that - just getting by.

■ Lack of Discipline

Discipline and disciple come from the same word. A wise teacher, when asked for a definition of character, replied, "Character is that quality which keeps us to our commitments long after the excitement of the moment in which that commitment was made is gone." How often, as college students, did you face an early-tomorrow-morning exam after an out-late-tonight party and promise yourself, "I'll get up early and study? I'm just too tired, now." Character is that which, when our feet hit that cold floor the next morning, causes us to continue rising.

Excitement will get you started, but discipline will keep you going long after the initial thrill has worn thin. The word "routine" has a negative meaning for many. Those who lack the discipline to stay with a task and see it through - those who bore easily with the present challenge - dislike the word, because it indicates repetition. Thoughtless repetition is self-defeating, but proactive, intentional discipline, which eventually becomes second nature, is the stuff which produces the "muscle" of strong leaders. Undisciplined leaders won't have followers - for long. "No retreat," that was our battle cry; "Semper Fi," that was our motto. I learned discipline as a young man logging pulp wood in Maine. Serving in the United States Marine Corps sealed the necessity of discipline. But being in ministry for 40 plus years has confirmed the blessing of discipline.

■ Refusal to Change

If we don't change, we don't grow. If we don't grow, we are not really living. The poet Robert Browning wrote, "Why stay we on the earth, except to grow?" All change is not growth, but all growth is change. The reality is, however, that all change can produce growth, if our reaction to that change is positive. Even more exciting is this revelation: Since change is inevitable, we can choose to be change agents, rather than reactors! Would you rather control the changes in your life or just wait around and try to adjust to whatever changes come your way? The equation, then, goes like this: *Action + Change + Growth = Life* <or> *Change + Inaction + Fear = Death.*

Growth can be terrifying, uncomfortable and cause a temporary loss of security, but without it, we die! Growth is a choice. It's the decision that makes all the difference.

■ Broken Trust

"Trust is the emotional glue that binds followers and leaders together" (Warren Bennis, *Leaders*). All the promises and all the schemes and all the motivating, challenging and inspiring words of great oratory may gather the crowds, but without trust, they will never lay any lasting foundation upon which something substantial can be built.

One of the unmade distinctions of the leader "wanna-be" is the difference between *attracting people* and *leading people*. Many charismatic and gifted men and women, with the ability to gather around them those who will listen, have been lured into the lie that they are in fact leading. Whether consciously or sub-consciously, these would-be leaders are operating in deception. When there is no real agenda other than to gather the crowd and impress them with great messages, eventually the listener feels betrayed. The trust that was given by their taking the time to hear the message is shattered by the realization that there is no movement behind the message. Words without the Walk. Verbiage without real Vision. Preaching but not Producing. Leading with no genuine leadership. Stage Talk, but no Walk. About the time these "leaders" sense growing frustration among their followers, they begin to hear God calling them to a new "set of ears."

Is it any wonder so many church members have the attitude that says, "We were here before you got here, and we'll be here when you're gone?" Leaders of the next millennium had better be willing to give their lives for the people God entrusts to them, and build with them a level of trust that flows out of unfailing commitment. Then, and only then, will we see followers become co-laborers who will match and even outrun us in covenant commitment to Kingdom and destiny. Build carefully and guard completely the trust level of your leadership. What is built over a <u>lifetime</u> can be destroyed in a <u>moment</u> of indiscretion!

■ Nearsighted Vision

"True leaders are always in the minority, because they are thinking ahead of the present majority. Even when the majority catches up, these leaders, as other leaders, will have moved ahead, and so again, will be in the minority." (Harry C. McKown, *A Boy Grows Up*).

One of the great examples of the importance of age and years of experience as an imperative resource for leadership is found right on the bridge of our nose. Those glasses that many of us in the over-forty crowd wear are tangible examples of the difference between near-sightedness and far-sightedness! As we grow older, it becomes easier for us to see things far away than up close. (Our memories as well, are more inclined toward the far away than the where-did-I-put-my-glasses, but that's another story)! The fact is, physical maturity brings about changes in our physical vision, and spiritual maturity provides us with the ability to focus on the big picture and be less moved by the fluctuations of the here-and-now.

Joseph survived the pettiness of his brothers, the pit of despair, the pretense of Potiphar's wife and the persecution of prison only because he was secure in the vision God had given him; A vision that was years away from fulfillment when it was given. Driving instructors teach novice car operators to focus on the farthest point at which they can see the road, while staying aware of closer objects through peripheral vision. Too much distraction by objects close on the right or the left can result in straying off the road. Dealing with the adjustments of the day-to-day, while focusing on the goal in the distance, is a quality all leaders possess.

FIVE SIGNPOSTS ON THE LEADERSHIP HIGHWAY
FIVE HABITS OF SUCCESSFUL LEADERSHIP

Signposts on the highway let us know we're going in the right direction. The signposts of leadership point to success in leading others to accomplish stated goals. Periodically, "reading" these signs in our lives and the lives of fellow leaders will keep us on course together.

1. INFLUENCE

We all are influencing others. The question is, how and for what purpose? People don't want to follow a leader because they have no choice. They want to choose to follow! It has been said that we are largely a product of the five people with whom we spend the most time. It has also been said that we will influence approximately 5000 people in our lifetime. While the average person may influence 5000 people in a lifetime in many organizations, leaders will influence 10s of thousands, even 100s of thousands. What is leadership, but influence?

Jesus spent the majority of His ministry with twelve carefully chosen men, among whom there was a definite inner core of three. The influence of these men spread, through the power of the Spirit, to over eight thousand with two sermons preached! Before His ascension, Jesus proclaimed to these men and the rest of the upper room assembly that they would receive power that would enable their influence to reach far beyond what His had been. That same power and that same influence is available to us today. The New Testament word for influence is "witness." "You shall witness to people in My name in Jerusalem, Judea, in Samaria, and then to the ends of the earth." Sounds to me like strong influence! What is the scope of your influence? The signpost of influence points to leadership.

2. PRIORITY

Activity is not necessarily accomplishment. It has been well said that the greatest enemy of the best is that which is good. We can get so bogged down by all the good that needs doing that we have no time or energy left for that which is best. Prioritizing our lives is an absolute necessity. First things must always be first things.

So many of God's people operate in a day-to-day, and even minute-to minute, crisis mode. Whatever we do next is the direct result of a particular voice being heard the loudest among a tumult of shouts. Why is it that we can be terribly busy with something on the "cutting edge" and when the phone rings, we stop to answer it, never knowing whether it represents another crisis or a telemarketer's sales pitch?

One of the subtle lies in the ears of God's Chosen is the making of, and checking off of, "to-do" lists as a measure of success. The fallacy of this trap is that we tend to make very subjective lists! In fact, we get so good at list-making that we can pencil dozens of ego boosting check-marks a day, without ever accomplishing anything of substance. We become very efficient without being effective. We do a lot, but we don't get a lot done. *"Deciding what not to do is just as important as deciding what to do"* (Archie Parrish.) The signpost of priority points to leadership.

3. VISION CASTING

In his book, *The Man Who Could Do No Wrong*, Charles Blair states his three points for sharing vision well:

1. What will be done?
2. How will you do it?
3. When will you begin?

Like a good reporter writing a story, the leader casting a vision must be able to articulate it well. If the vision is valid but the words are weak, the fire may flicker, but it won't flame very high, and it won't ignite much around it, either. In order to effectively share the "fire" within, we need to understand the difference between burden and vision and between vision and the visionary.

Burden is on the inside. Vision is on the outside. Vision is what we see ourselves doing about the burden within. A visionary only dreams about doing something, but a person with a vision actually does something about it!

> **A vision without a mission makes a visionary. A mission without a vision is drudgery. But a vision with a mission and a mission that has vision makes a missionary. And missionaries are relentless.**

Jim Rohn, author of the Treasury of Quotes, notes, *"In order to accomplish our dreams, we must eventually wake up!"* The world is full of dreamers, but finding "doers" is rare. We can only do a little if we are doing it by ourselves. The key to great accomplishment is the attraction of others to the work. If our vision is not articulated there is no opportunity for others to join us. If it is not attractive no one wants to.

Finally, the casting of vision must contain simple and direct steps for those who wish to serve the vision to do so. Finding a vision compelling and discovering a personal place in it are not the same thing. Many visionaries make their dreams attractive while never providing opportunity or direction for others to become involved. Perhaps #4 in Blair's steps to vision casting should be, *"How can I be involved?"* The signpost of vision-casting points to leadership.

4. DECISION MAKING

The ability to make decisions is imperative to leadership. What keeps most people from being good decision makers is that they think they must be great decision makers. Read the sentence again: The ability to make decisions is imperative to leadership. Did you read that sentence with a certain adjective inserted? The ability to make decisions, not the ability to make right decisions one hundred percent of the time, or even the ability to make right decisions fifty-one percent of the time, but simply the ability to make decisions. Fear of making the wrong decision, which results in making no decision, is *worse* than making the wrong decision! Ask any successful leader and see if they didn't make many wrong decisions along the way before eventually making some right. What separates them from the crowd of ordinary folk is that they were willing to risk being wrong in order to have the *opportunity* to be right!

Several years ago, Herbert Green stood on the final hole of the

U.S. Open Golf Championship with only a twenty-two inch putt left to win. In the pressure of the moment he hit the ball too softly, left it short of the hole - and himself short of golf history. His ability to speak philosophically of that day (some months later) resulted in one of the great quotes of the game of golf: *"Ninety percent of all putts that stop short of the hole never go in."* If Herbert would allow us to borrow that analogy, we can say with some assurance that ninety percent of those who never make decisions will never make a good decision! The adage, "Do something, even if it's wrong," has it's place, as long as we eventually get it right. Dealing with the fear of the consequences of our decisions leads to another observation:

Our problems are not our problem! Our problem is not knowing what to do with our problems. We get stalled with paralysis of analysis. Prayer, counsel and research have their place. Pray, seek advice, study, and then make a firm, decisive step in the direction seen as best and be willing to deal with the consequences. Take the blame, defer the praise, and face the next decision with the last one "under your belt!" One of my mentors told me years ago, "Paul, the most important thing you need to know is the very next thing to do. And the most important thing to do is that." The signpost of decision-making points to leadership.

5. PEOPLE BUILDING

We don't build great churches, companies or organizations, we build great people who will build great enterprises! There are no small churches, no big churches, only stagnant people and growing people! If we have stagnant people, no matter how big our church is now, it will drop to the level of our stagnation. No matter how small our organization is now, if it is filled with growth-minded people, it will not stay small for long.

Again, Jesus poured His life into a relatively small group of men and women. He could have attracted a crowd any time He wished, and on more than one occasion, even when He didn't want to. He chose, however, to train, equip and empower a team of followers whom He knew would become powerful leaders in time. He also knew that the intensity of His vision would eventually thin out the crowd - and it did! To those in whom He had invested the most He asked, "Will you also go away?" The proof of leadership was in Peter's answer, "Where would we go? You only have the words of life." Are we building a team with that kind of commitment?

SOME BIBLE LEADERS WHO FAILED ... BUT THEY WERE NOT FAILURES!

Learn the difference between truth and fact. The facts may say you failed, but the Truth is, *you are not a failure!*

1. *Moses*: Failed when he struck down an Egyptian, and later when he struck the rock, but we remember him as the meekest man on the earth, and the great lawgiver.
2. *Abraham:* Failed when he lied about his wife, but we remember him as the father of the faithful.
3. *Samson*: Failed because of the sins of the flesh, but we remember him as the strong man who pulled down Philistine strongholds.
4. *David*: Failed with Bathsheba, but is remembered as the Man after the heart of God, and the father of Solomon, the wisest and most powerful king to live on the earth.
5. *Elijah*: Failed in his encounter with Jezebel but is known as one of the most powerful prophets who ever lived and who left Elisha to take his place; a man of the double portion anointing.
6. *Peter*: Failed the love test, the loyalty test, and spent more

time with his foot in his mouth than any other Apostle, but stood up on the day of Pentecost and preached the gospel with three thousand souls coming into the kingdom.

7. *Paul*: Failed, wanted to quit in Corinth; was constantly reminded of his past but is considered the greatest Christian who ever lived. He wrote two-thirds of the New Testament.

"Failure is not final if you have faith to finish" —*Paul Tsika*

Learn the John Mark Principle

1. **STARTED OUT GREAT.** Part of the missionary team of Paul and Barnabas. (Acts 12:25)

2. **LEFT THE TEAM.** We don't know all the reasons, but it looked like he quit! (Acts 15:37-39)

3. **CAUSED A SPLIT BETWEEN TWO GREAT MEN:** Paul and Barnabas. (Acts 15:39)

4. **RESTORED AND USEFUL.** "Get Mark and bring him with you, for he is useful to me for ministry." (2Timothy 4:11)

5. **SAW THE RELATIONSHIP BETWEEN PAUL AND BARNABAS RESTORED.**

He Turned His Failure into Success! And You Can Too!

CHAPTER 4

Beware of the Vision Stealers
...They Are Everywhere!

Duke Ellington, the late jazz musician and renowned band leader, was once asked to provide a definition of rhythm. *"If you got it,"* he replied, *"You don't need no definition. And if you don't have it, ain't no definition gonna help."*

> **Vision: Once you have it, you know it, but when you don't, you aren't quite sure what it looks like.**

A good working definition from George Barna's book, *The Power of Vision* has helped me considerably: "You might define vision as *foresight* with *insight* based on *hindsight.*" Everyone seems to have a definition of vision. Here's what a few others have said.

> **'Vision' is:**
> **...Seeing the invisible and making it visible.**
> **... an informed bridge from the present to the future.**
> **... Sanctified Dreams.**

Here's one from George Barna that will work for us: *"Vision: A mental image of a preferable future imparted by God to His chosen servants and is based upon an accurate understanding of God, self, and circumstances."*

Let's break Barna's definition down with an application from Joshua five and six.

A Mental Image (Joshua 6: 2) *"And the Lord said to Joshua: See! I have given Jericho into your hand; it's king, and the mighty men of valor."*

Question: *What did God want Joshua to see?* As he stood before Jericho, the walls were just as impregnable as they had always been! God was imparting something to Joshua. It was a vision of the future. *His* future.

What mental image do you have of your destiny? If it is an image conjured by wishes and hopes, tremendous frustration will follow. If, however, it is an image of the will of God, it cannot fail. Since time isn't an issue with God, He is able to say to us, "See (present tense)! I have given (completed action) *your enemies* into your hand" (Italics mine).

A Preferable Future (Joshua 6:5) *"...the wall of the city will fall down flat!"*

Of course, that was the desired result. Joshua couldn't do it by his own schemes, designs or plans. It had to come from God. Real vision always produces desired results. The hard part is giving up our *good* ideas for *God's* ideas. Again, someone has well said, "The worst enemy of that which is best is that which is good." If we are to see a preferable future, we must be willing to set aside all the things that interfere with God's *best* plan, even though some of those things may be very good. God hasn't called any of us to omnipotence - that's His area.

Traditionally, leaders, especially church leaders, have been expected to be all things to all people. Thousands of men and women leave ministry positions each year, toasted to a crisp by the expectations of those around them. We need to be focused (not narrow-minded) on *our* vision, enabled by *our* gifting, in order to conquer *our* foes, to see the walls of *our* opposition fall down flat!

Those in the business community experience the same challenges but have the same solutions, we may tire in the work but we never tire of the work when it comes from God.

Imparted by God (Joshua 6:2) *". . . the Lord said."*

Joshua had been walking around those walls, no doubt trying to find some way for this thing to happen. It was only when God showed up that he had the way to accomplish what God told him to do earlier (Joshua 1). Quite possibly, as you read this, you may be thinking, "I've seen the thing that God has shown me. I've sold out to The Plan. I'm ready to accomplish what God has revealed, but *I don't have a clue how to do it!"* Be assured, fellow leader, that God has a plan and you shall soon know it. The vision of God, to the people of God, of the plan of God, is always accompanied by the power of God. The full comprehension of God's plan is based upon: **An accurate understanding of God, self and circumstances.** (Joshua 5:13-15)

Of God (Joshua 5:14) *"...Commander of the Army...."*

He didn't come to take sides but to take over. There is only one way God operates in our destiny. God! In charge! His way! Without limitation! Sorry, God is not anyone's co-pilot. He's not a partner, and He's not a consultant. When God came to Joshua, He came as the unquestioned Supreme Commander. If and when He shows up at our place, there might as well be no conditions or restraints as to how, when or even why He does what He does. True understanding of God is based upon the realization that He hardly ever moves as we want or expect Him to move! Are we willing to accept Him on His terms? He sometimes shows up as a Marine on steroids with a flame thrower and burns up all our plans.

Of Self (Joshua 5:14) *"...fell on his face to the earth and worshiped, ..."*

What a relief it was, when Joshua realized that taking Jericho was not his responsibility but God's! We can almost feel the emotion in Joshua's response. Falling down before the presence of the Lord can be as much a sign of relief as worship! Ever been in that place where, if God didn't show up, all is lost? Everything that we can do has been done and victory is still far away? Certainly, Joshua was worshiping. At the Word of God he removes his shoes. His first words to the Lord, however, reveal his upper-most thoughts: "What saith the Lord...?" God, in order to be God, will allow us to come to the end of ourselves and realize that we *must* have Him. Don't be guilty of the response of one church leader who, when told it was time to pray about a difficult situation, exclaimed, "Has it come to that?"

Of Circumstances (Joshua 6:1) *"... Jericho was securely shut up ..."*

During this whole experience Joshua was having a major reality check. Can you imagine what it was like as he got back to camp and told them he had God's plan (vision) for taking the city? They all knew this was an impossible situation: green troops, never really tested in battle, and a leader who was just as inexperienced as they were. Joshua comes back, calls everyone together and declares, "I have a vision from God! Here is what we are going to do. We will march around the city once a day for six days, and seven times on the seventh day, shout real loud, blow some trumpets and the walls will fall down. And, by the way, we're going to let the praise team lead the way." By this time, they were beginning to form a pulpit search committee; The pastor has lost his mind! Joshua is about to find out - *the future ain't what it used to be.*

> When God begins to impart vision, what should our response be? The fact is, there are Vison Stealers from within and without ready to steal what God has put in our hearts.

HOLD FAST!

Hebrews 10:23 tells us, *"Let us hold fast the confession of our faith without wavering (for He is faithful that promised)."* The key word here is the one translated *hold fast.* In Greek, the word is *katecho,* a combination of two root words, *kata,* and *echo.* Kata carries the idea of something coming downward, something that comes down so hard, so heavily, that it is overpowering, dominating, even subjugating. When this force arrives on the scene, it conquers, it subdues and it immediately brings influencing power. Echo is a word which means "I have" and carries the notion of possession. This is a picture of someone who has sought for something for a long time. After finally finding the object of their dreams, and joyfully running toward it, they embrace it, hold it and declare, "It's finally mine!" When *kata* and *echo* are compounded into *kataecho,* it means to "embrace tightly." The phrase, "hold fast," is so strong it can actually be translated to "suppress."

What a description of the *strong* response to the will of God for our lives when His plan begins to come alive in our souls, and we realize exactly what we are called to do. We must "hold fast" the vision God has spoken into our lives. We must wrap our arms around it and place all our "weight" on it. Why? The vision stealers are everywhere!

> The Vision Stealers want to take what God has placed in our spirits. In so doing, they will rob us of our individual purpose in His wonderful plan!

Vision Stealers — From Within

Complacency

Far too many believers settle for the lie of the enemy called "Average." We cannot settle for being average when God has called us to a "first class" life! Some fail to behave with passion because of ignorance or complacency. "It doesn't matter what we do - God will bless our efforts," is the attitude of a half-baked, half-blessed life. He <u>does</u> care what we do. Complacency is the extinguisher of our passion, hence our vision. The primary goal of our efforts to assist people in finding destiny and purpose is to determine their passion-point. We ask, "What is it that you feel so strongly about that your pulse quickens, your mind works overtime, and you feel the urge to pound your fist on the table when the subject comes up?" "What will you argue about quickly?" These and similar questions reveal our passions, which lead to vision when God directs our lives! We need to realize that the objective of the Enemy is not to get us to hate - it is to keep us from caring deeply. In fact, the opposite of love is not hate; the opposite of both love and hate is apathy. Complacency is a vision stealer.

Fear

Vision requires change and change means breaking out of the comfort zone, doing new things and operating in areas in which we lack a track record of success. Change can produce fear! There is a saying we use in this area: "New levels - New Devils!" Conquering new heights always means conquering new fears. On the other hand, trying and failing can produce fear as well.

> **"Sometimes we are overcome by fear, because we have failed in the past and dare not reach for the stars again." (Barna)**

For the most part fear is in perception not in reality. Job's confession, "That which I greatly feared has come upon me," is the result of the biblical principle of confession. Say something long enough, loud enough and often enough, and it will tend to happen. Most of us spend far too much time confessing the very thing we don't want to happen! Let something adverse occur, and we confess, "Just my luck," or "I knew that was going to happen," or "I always do that." What a way to live, so let's face change with the sure knowledge that fear will try to deter and be ready with the positive confession of faith. Fear is a vision stealer. Confesss your faith not your fears.

False
Evidence
Appearing
Real

"For God has not given us a spirit of fear, but
of power and of love and of a sound mind."
(2Timothy 1:7)

Tradition

This is one of the most popular and devastating barriers to true vision. This is *"The notion that God would never cause you to change what you have always done"* (Barna). God can and does use tradition to provide a semblance of consistency and stability in life, but He has absolutely no use for traditions that block progress. "I've never done it this way before," is the battle cry of many people of faith. Tradition is a reflection of the past while Vision is a reflection of the future. God is not the author of confusion. So don't doubt in the dark what God has shown you in the light. And don't let a tradition that has lost its power to move you to action become your golden calf. Tradition can be a vision stealer.

Fatigue

When fatigue enters and we begin to lose focus, we open ourselves up to the Enemy to erode the vision God has given us. We need to learn the difference between being tired and being fatigued. We all get tired. In fact, if we never get tired, we never gain stamina. To build a muscle, athletes first tire the muscle, and then allow it to rest. It is in the resting after use that the muscle becomes stronger. Fatigue is that level of tiredness for which normal amounts of rest are ineffective. We can't seem to "bounce back" like we did before. Stress is not an enemy. Stress from which there are not frequent and consistent periods of relief is the killer. Take a vacation! Jesus took time off. Who do you think you are? Fatigue is a vision stealer.

> "But they that wait upon the Lord shall
> renew their strength; they shall mount up
> with wings as eagles; they shall run, and not
> be weary; and they shall walk, and not faint."
> (Isaiah 40:31)

Stagnation

Stagnation occurs when we do not remain in "motion" with our God-given vision. There are too many "Dead Sea Christians." They are taking in and never giving out! We mustn't get hooked on yesterday's glory and success and let stagnation rob us of tomorrow's dreams. Einstein discovered one of God's creation principles when he wrote $E=MC^2$. Objects at rest tend to stay at rest, and objects in motion tend to stay in motion. Why would this be any less true in the Spiritual realm than in the natural realm? Whatever is true in the natural is generally *more* true in the Spirit. How is your business momentum? Stagnation is a vision stealer.

Sloth

One of the most dangerous conditions of all is slothfulness. Sloth means "a disinclination to action or labor." You can be "busy" and still have it! This is a demonic spirit and must be dealt with.

> *"That ye be not slothful, but followers of them who through faith and patience inherit the promises."* (Hebrews 6:12)

Write this out and read this often. Never has there been a greater description of a Lazy Loser in Life (LLL).

> *"I went by the field of the slothful, and by the vineyard of the man void of understanding; And, lo, it was all grown over with thorns, and nettles had covered the face thereof, and the stone wall thereof was broken down. Then I saw, and considered it well: I looked upon it, and received instruction. Yet a little sleep, a little slumber, a little folding of the hands to sleep: So shall thy poverty come as one that travelleth; and thy want as an armed man."* (Proverbs 24:30-34)

> *"Slothfulness casteth into a deep sleep; and an idle soul shall suffer hunger."* (Proverbs 19:15)

Vision Stealers — From Without

Time

Time is a neutral force. It can work for us or against us. Time can be a healing force or a destructive force. As time passes and our vision remains unfulfilled, we begin to hear a voice saying, "Don't waste anymore of your time, it's not going to happen for you. You probably didn't really get a word from God." We kill time, waste time, spend time, and lose time, when all the while the scripture admonishes us to *"Redeem the time, for the days are evil . . . "* (Eph. 5:16.) *"Humble yourselves therefore under the mighty hand of God, that He may exalt you in due time"* (1Peter 5:6). I challenge you to chart how you spend your time over the course of this next week. What takes most of your time? Wasted time is a vision stealer.

Satan

If time doesn't cause us to lose our vision, then we will hear the condemning voice of the adversary ringing in our ears. Remember, he is the Accuser of the Brethren. The Enemy will attack us at the point of our identity in Christ. The same dragon that waited to snatch away the Savior at birth (Revelation 12:4) stands at the delivery room of our vision, and he is hungry! He will try to convince us that our vision is nothing more than an ego trip, and that in order to be really humble, we must be and do nothing in the Kingdom. That's not what the Bible says!

> *"For we are His workmanship, created in Christ Jesus for good works, which God prepared beforehand that we should walk in them."* (Ephesians 2:10)

Satan is *the* vision stealer.

Friends

When wasted time and even Satan himself have failed to steal our vision, we often face one of the most insidious and effective of all thieves. Friends will come and help you gain a "balanced perspective." There are friends who are comforting and helpful, to be sure, but there are others who know us for what we are and always have been. They can't see us any other way. Our vision threatens them, especially if *they* are living mundane and mediocre lives for the Lord. Well meaning friends can often bring terribly negative perspectives to our vision. Negativity is one of the trademarks of the operation of the flesh, and flesh never will believe God or His word. It looks for the worst in every situation. Acts 5:38-39 is pretty good advice for those who would "wet-blanket" anyone's vision: Friends *can be* vision stealers.

> *"And now I say unto you, Refrain from*
> *these men, and let them alone: for if this*
> *counsel or this work be of men, it will come*
> *to nought: But if it be of God, ye cannot*
> *overthrow it; lest haply ye be found even to*
> *fight against God."*

Family

The final challenge is usually the most difficult and oftentimes painful, because it could come from your own family. Time can be redeemed, the Devil can be rebuked, and we can tell our friends, "Good-bye," but we always have our family. This is so personal! More than anyone else in the world, our family knows all of our faults. Joseph knew this truth well: *"Now Joseph had a dream, and he told it to his brothers; and they hated him even more"* (Genesis 37:5). Families are *often* vision stealers.

This Is Important:

No matter how long it takes; no matter
how many times you have to tell the Devil
to "shut up;" no matter how many of your
"friends" call you crazy; no matter how it
hurts when your family comes against you,
hold fast to the vision God has placed in
your heart!

INTERDEPENDENCE NOT INDEPENDENCE

One of the greatest deterrents against vision stealers is
community. So I want to end this chapter with Eight Functions of
Community That will Empower You to Success.

Team Work (A Sense of Belonging)

Oneness in Responsibilities (A Sense of Bonding)

Giving and Forgiving (A Sharing of Burdens)

Edification (A Sharing of Blessings)

Teaching (A Setting Forth of the Basics)

Holding Yourself Accountable (A Sense of Body Life)

Evangelism (A Sharing of Beliefs)

Reproduction (Duplicating What We Believe)

LET'S GET STARTED!
Are you ready to map your vision course?

CHAPTER 5

Mapping Your Destiny
Your Roadmap to Success

"Trust in the LORD with all thine heart; and lean not unto thine own understanding. In all thy ways acknowledge him, and he shall direct thy paths." (Proverbs 3:5-6)

God is God of purpose: His and ours; His through ours and ours through His. If we are to be people of destiny, it is absolutely essential that we find the purpose of God, and then discover His intentions for us to accomplish what He desires. Our paths must be His paths. Our purpose must be His purpose. The writer of Proverbs tells us that God has fore-ordained certain paths or highways we are to travel and has promised to direct us along the way.

When I begin planning for a trip along a route I have never traveled, I often will consult AAA Travel Services who will prepare a trip plan including my route, resources along the way such as fuel, food and rest areas, and an estimation of the time needed for the trip. My part is to simply follow the plan. This proved to be very helpful, especially when Billie and I traveled in our Prevost Bus for years. Now we have Google maps. As God begins to reveal His plan for our destiny, we need to be aware of our contribution to the success of the journey.

First, I am to *trust Him*. What good would it do to ask for help from AAA if I did not confidently believe that they knew the best way? In our pursuit of purpose, it is an easy thing to *say* we trust the

Lord, but do we really? There have been times when my actions have shown that I am not fully convinced of His trustworthiness. Some trust is actually no trust. We are told to trust *"with all our hearts."* We will never fully realize our potential for Kingdom purpose until the trust issue is settled once and for all. When vision is from God, it is big. When vision is big, it is scary. When vision is scary, it's difficult to "let go" and trust His way. What is there that God might ask us to do that we would find it hard to trust completely to Him?

Second, I must submit to a *higher understanding*. AAA is an international organization with resources vastly superior to mine. They have access to up-to-date highway information, road conditions, and even weather situations which might affect the trip. Why is it then, that I have no trouble submitting to their understanding of the best way to go, but I often believe that I know better than God how to travel in the Spirit!?! It's preposterous, isn't it? God doesn't expect us to throw our brain away, but the fact remains that our intellect is often the worst enemy of our ability to tap into a supernatural understanding of our destiny highway. We don't quit thinking, we simply submit our mind to His mind.

Third, I am to *acknowledge Him*. The Hebrew word is *Yada*, which means to know - or more literally to comprehend by seeing. As I am following my AAA route to my physical destination, I would be foolish to keep my eyes glued constantly to the directions and not the road! Furthermore, as good as an AAA trip plan may be, I would be far better served if I were privileged to have the person who designed the route to lead me. If our eyes are constantly on the terrain in front of us or the map in our lap, we will never be as confident as when we focus on the one who knows the way! Destiny is as much the journey as it is the destination, and our eyes must be on the Lord of our lives, not on our lives.

Nehemiah's Plan

Nehemiah was a planner. He knew how to "map" his destiny highway. As God burdened his heart with the ruined state of the city, He also began to give Nehemiah a plan for it's restoration.

> **Remember: Burden is what we feel strongly about—**
> **Vision is what we see ourselves doing about it.**

Let's examine the steps, or "roads," Nehemiah took to accomplish his vision.

■ **Vision is imparted.**

> *"And it came to pass, when I heard these words, that I sat down and wept, and mourned certain days, and fasted, and prayed before the God of heaven."*
> (Nehemiah 1:4)

Nehemiah heard the report, and he was deeply moved. He began to weep. Then he began to fast and pray. This man was serious about the situation! He came to the point where he could think of nothing other than the need before him. Learn the lesson of Nehemiah: vision is often borne of crisis.

■ **Vision is "cast."**

> *"And I said unto the king, If it please the king, and if thy servant has found favour in thy sight, that thou wouldest send me unto Judah, unto the city of my fathers' sepulchres, that I may build it."* (Nehemiah 2:5)

When Nehemiah had personally prepared himself through prayer and fasting, he was ready to share his vision with someone who had the resources to help him accomplish it. We are fond of dreamily telling those who can't do anything about our plans, "If only I knew how to go about it, I would . . . ." Nehemiah knew it would take great resources to accomplish his purpose, and he knew only one man who could give him what he needed.

■ **Strategy is given.**

> *"And the king said unto me, (the queen also sitting by him,) 'For how long shall thy journey be? And when wilt thou return?' So it pleased the king to send me; and I set him a time."* (Nehemiah 2:6)

Knowing the right resources will never accomplish our task; we must eventually *ask* those who can help. What bright young entrepreneur would *think* of approaching a prospect to sponsor without a thorough business plan presented convincingly and with passion? Verses 6 and following are the account of Nehemiah's "business plan," complete with resources needed and a time for it's implementation . . . .

■ **Vision becomes reality.**

> *"Then Eliashib the high priest rose up with his brethren the priests, and they builded the sheep gate; they sanctified it, and set up the doors of it; even unto the tower of Meah they sanctified it, unto the tower of Hananeel."* (Nehemiah 3:1)

Here's where many a vision falls to the ground unfulfilled. The groaning and praying are over, the planning and strategy are set, the resources are in place, and then — THE HARD WORK BEGINS! We read in the verses following all the assignments and all the tasks, each group to their own particular job, but the most telling phrase of the account is chapter four, verse six: (*"For the people had a mind to work"*). In just *52 days* it was done (Nehemia 6:15)! The next verse is the verse of victory: *"And it came to pass, that when all our enemies heard thereof, and all the heathen that were about us saw these things, they were much cast down in their own eyes: for they perceived that this work was wrought of our God."*

THE IMPORTANCE OF WRITTEN GOALS

Most of us take more time planning our annual vacation than we do planning our lives. We have plans for our houses, plans for our social life, plans for our retirement and great plans for our children, but we just never seem to have time to consider our own personal goals. The question before us is this: What are we doing today that will insure that we will not be doing the same thing five years from now?

In the great children's classic, *Alice in Wonderland*, we hear this exchange between Alice and the Cheshire Cat:

ALICE: Mr. Cat, which of these paths shall I take?

CAT: Well, my dear, where do you want to go?

ALICE: I don't suppose it really matters.

CAT: Then, my dear, any path will do!

Think of someone who is successful and effective in their chosen field of endeavor. Is it at all possible they got to where they are by following "any path?" Did any of these people become who they are by saying, "I don't suppose it really matters?"

In a national survey, *Time Magazine* found that only three percent of respondents had any written goals. Ninety-seven percent of Americans either had not thought about writing goals or had never found the time. The interesting portion of the survey report was this: The three percent who had written goals had accomplished more than all the other ninety-seven percent! If that isn't shocking enough, personal success and motivational speaker Brian Tracy's research shows that the act of simply writing goals *triples* the likelihood that they will become reality.

Why is it then, that more of us aren't grabbing pencil and paper this very minute? The evidence is overwhelming, but the majority remain unmoved. Let me suggest four reasons by giving them names.

■ **Vance the Victim**

Vance is quick to explain his lack of planning because his lot is determined by things beyond his control. His past has imprisoned him in a predetermined, perpetual poverty, and his present has been stolen by parents, politicians or teachers! Any excuse for failing will do, and anyone is likely to be the bad guy. If everyone else *would* do what they *should* do, Vance's life would fall into place.

■ **Paul the Procrastinator**

Paul is the guy who has forgotten the past and never worries about the future. He lives for the "here and now." He loves the way things are at the moment. He will do almost anything to maintain the status quo: Avoid change at all costs. The only plans he makes are to make sure things stay just as they are. Paul doesn't attempt anything, because his fear is not of failing but of *success.* He is afraid he cannot *be* the person he must *become* in order to do the things it takes to succeed. He simply doesn't believe God could make him that man.

■ Don the Dreamer

Don loves to plan! In fact, most of his time is spent planning. He has notebooks of notions, folders filled with formulas and a brain full of big ideas. He loves to tell anyone within earshot about his latest and best concepts and will talk for an eternity without ever really getting anything done. Don, you see, is not willing to pay the price of putting dreams into action. There is a price tag on success, but Don knows that talk is cheap.

■ Freddie the Focused

Freddie is the guy who knows that the past is not to be lived in — only learned from. He also knows that the present is all he is promised and all he has to work with right now. He spends his time wisely doing everything he can to maximize his potential. He is busy developing integrity and character and honing his gifts to a fine razor's edge. The reason he is accomplishing so much today is that he spent a portion of yesterday in prayerful planning. As a result, he is clear about his purpose, growing toward his potential and sowing seeds today with an eye on his promised harvest to come.

What makes Freddie different? The answer is simple: He has clear, written goals. Some believe that goals are ungodly; that anything short of "flowing in the Spirit" is humanism and fleshly selfishness. If we aren't disconnected, dreamy-eyed and "Hangin' with the Holy Ghost," we aren't really spiritual. There's a Greek word in scripture for that kind of thinking: HOGWASH! God is the most organized, proactive and deliberate Being alive. To be sure, there are times to set aside the "order of service" and allow God to move in exciting, even surprising ways. In the middle of His plan for our lives, there will be unexpected, creative interludes. We must remember, though, that they are only unexpected to us, never to Him. God never operates in the "spur of the moment." He never surprises Himself!

For the Believer, then, our goals are a result of discerning the present and future plan of God, and aligning our lives with that plan. I like to call them "sanctified goals."

WHAT WILL SANCTIFIED GOALS DO?

➤ *Give us a sense of purpose.*

When we set a goal that is in line with the will of God for our lives, a light goes on in our future! We now have a focus point that positively impacts our actions. Even when it is dark around us, we are never very far off course. Our present position is accurately known, and our course is true.

➤ *Keep us moving.*

Goals provide motivation. Each small sub-goal attained is a shot of spiritual adrenaline which produces greater motivation for the next. Motivation becomes momentum, and momentum sustained will make the speed bumps indiscernible. A small impediment on a train track will keep a train at rest from moving forward, but a locomotive at full speed will plow through concrete walls with ease!

➤ *Determine our priorities.*

All the motivation and momentum in the world is less than useless if it is wasted on things that aren't contributing to reaching our destination. Sanctified goals keep us pointed in the right direction doing things that are important. Remember, the greatest enemy of that which is best is that which is good. Goals keep us involved in God's best for our lives. Goals help us separate the essential from the trivial.

➤ *Become destiny's mile-markers.*

God's revelation of Himself to His people is progressive. He shows

Himself and His plan in incremental fashion. If He didn't, we couldn't take it! Our goals, as well, should be progressive and measurable. Like mile-markers on a highway, each goal met is an indicator of how far we've come and how far we must go. Airlines recognize the need for indicating progress. On overseas flights especially, there is constant and consistent information as to elapsed time, time remaining, air speed and distance to destination. Measurable goals provide incentives to continued success.

> *Remember: Success is not a destination, but a journey. The key to reaching our potential lies in continual improvement, not being perfect all the time. Don't buy the lie that activity equals advancement or that exertion means excellence. Jim Rohn, who has been called the "Sage of Success" says, "Excellence is a worthy pursuit, not because of what it will get you, but because of what it will* make *of you."*

Let's look at the process of creating our own personal roadmap from inception to success:

Burden turns to Vision
Vision leads to Goal-setting
Goals map our Actions
Actions create Results
Consistent Results is called Success!

The alternative to this process is to live like the ninety-seven percent who generally aim at nothing, and hit it with amazing accuracy! Henry Ford said, "Whether you think you can or you think you can't, you are right."

"OK," you say, "I'm convinced. How do I begin to map my personal destiny? I know I need to set sanctified goals and begin to live like I have a plan, but how do I know what goals are right for me?"

Let's look at the example of Moses in Exodus three. Moses took a big leap in his life's purpose when he went from the desert to become the deliverer of the Hebrew people. What can we learn from his experience?

MOSES HAD A SENSE OF HIS CREATION PURPOSE (VISION)

From his birth, it was evident that God was preparing Moses for some special task. His rescue, up-bringing, and education in Pharoah's palace was not an accident. Long before the burning bush, we see that Moses knew deep inside that he was created to be a leader. When the Egyptian was beating his countryman, Moses intervened, but because he was acting in his own power, it went terribly wrong and ended in murder (Exodus 2:11). The next day, he attempts to arbitrate a disagreement between two Hebrew men (Exodus 2:13). Later, in Midian, he helps the women when they are driven from the well by the shepherds (Exodus 2:16).

Every one of us is created for a purpose as great as that of Moses! If we ever get that truth to hit home in our self-concept, there will be trouble in the kingdom of darkness. Satan is successful in convincing the vast majority (at least ninety-seven percent) of us that it's just not true. "Not for me, anyway. Maybe someone else. Maybe even *everyone* else, but not me." Without a God-given vision of who we are and what we are created to do, we will wind up like Moses. His very creation purpose, taken into his own hands, made him a murderer instead of a leader. "I've tried to be what I believe God called me to be," you say, "And it has gone all wrong." I'm sure Moses was repeating that same thought as he sat by a well in a strange land using his gifting and calling as a leader to moderate petty arguments over who would drink instead of marching ahead of millions of people as they found their way to freedom. I'm sure he wondered if he had permanently "blown it." I imagine he doubted whether God even knew his address. As Moses was about to find out, God never rescinds His calling on our lives (Romans 11:29) and He knows *exactly* where we are at every moment. His gifts and callings are without repentance. God doesn't change His mind about His purpose for you.

Moses' Vision is Clarified by God

As Moses tended sheep on the back of the desert, God intervened. Notice, he wasn't just *in* the desert but on the *back-side* of the desert. Ever been Pastor of that church? In the presence of God, Moses worshiped, was renewed, and reclaimed his vision and calling. The presence of Almighty God is like that. When He comes into our situation, it doesn't matter how far back in the desert we've been. We receive all that we need to get on with our purpose. The first step to mapping our personal destiny is an encounter with the *Living God.* Already saved, you say? Wonderful. In full time service? Fabulous. Important denominational committees? Lovely. Been there, done that, and still knew the back-side of the desert intimately. Until and unless we are willing to turn aside to the presence of God, take off our shoes in worship, and receive the "now" Word of God for our circumstances, we will wake up every morning to the hot sand and the smell of sheep. Talked to any burning bushes lately?

The second step to a well-mapped destiny is learning not to argue with God. What? Argue with God? Yes, and quite regularly, too. Sometimes we don't even realize we are doing it, but we argue. In fact, every time we sense the Spirit urging us to do something, and we don't immediately do it, we are arguing with God. Moses did it as well as anyone ever has:

Who has sent me? (Exodus 3:13) This objection is really a crisis of *authority*, and it must be answered in our lives as well. If we are hesitating to respond to the call of God, the underlying issue is whether or not we really believe Jehovah God is in it! He is just as much our "I Am" as he was Moses'.

They won't believe me. (Exodus 4:1) Moses' second objection was a crisis of *authenticity*. He knew the Israelite Nation believed in God, he just wasn't convinced they would believe him. God was prepared to authenticate His call on Moses' life, but He would do it through that which Moses already possessed - his shepherd's rod. God took what Moses had, added His supernatural power, and told Moses to use it to glorify Him. God's question still rings in the ears of those who struggle with the crisis of authenticity. "What's in your hand?"

I am not eloquent. (Exodus 4:10) This objection is a crisis of *articulation*. We think of articulation as the ability of excellent verbal expression, but that is actually a secondary meaning of the word. Webster's primary definition is, "The joint between bones or cartilages - the action or manner of jointing or interrelating." Moses inner fear was that he would be unable to adequately bring God's people back into relationship with Him. God's response to Moses and to us is, "I made your mouth, and I will be with your mouth!" (See Exodus 4:11,12)

Others can do better. Moses' final objection (he dared not bring another, for God was getting weary of them) is the crisis of *assurance*. "Lord, are you absolutely positive that I'm the one to do this?" Through the years of ministry, I have often known people who want to fill a particular position, knowing they really wanted to be used in that area, only to hear them say, "Are you sure so-and-so wouldn't be better?" We all want to know that we have been chosen because we are God's first choice, not because everyone else was too busy. The realization that, out of all the universe, God wants *us* for the job is amazing! Why did God get angry at this objection? When we defer our calling because we think someone else could do it better, we are simply confessing our lack of trust in Him.

At the end of the day, all Moses' objections were simply an expression of his insecurity. Sometimes our self-deprecation is a veiled desire for someone to encourage us and tell us that we *are* equal to the task. When God says we can — WE CAN! With this kind of confidence, we can begin to set sanctified goals in earnest.

WRITE YOUR PURPOSE STATEMENT

If only three percent of Americans have written goals, even fewer have written and adopted a personal purpose or mission statement. A purpose statement is a simple, concise description of life purpose and calling. It is specific, progressive and clear. It should be no more than three or four sentences. Any more than that means more work is needed to refine and focus life goals.

Right now is a good time to close this book, get pen and paper and start working on the first draft. Purpose statements are refined and fine-tuned from time to time but change very little in their essential nature. Ask the Holy Spirit to speak and trust that God will guide in the process. Billie and I have a simple mission statement that defines our purpose. Here it is:

> **To impact our generation for generations to come with the truth of God's Word. Glorifying God in word and in deed and to hear "well done" at life's end.**

WRITING GOALS

Since goals are born from our life purpose and mission, we can now begin the process of outlining and writing them. Eventually, we want to have a year plan, a five year plan, and a ten year plan. Here are a few guidelines:

Write them down. You have a photographic memory? Write them down anyway! The weakest ink is better than the strongest memory.

Make them personal. This is not the time to wax eloquently, grandiose and flowery. Be *real.* Remember, you are talking to yourself, so use language you can understand!

Be specific. Vague and general goals are often comfortable, but not at all useful. Good goals virtually spell out the resources necessary for completion. Get into the details. Many small specific goals are better than a few hazy concepts.

Make them time-sensitive. Someone has said that goals are dreams with deadlines. Every good goal has a completion date attached. If circumstances beyond control force changes, modify completion dates without guilt. Otherwise, *stick to the plan.*

Make them measurable. List, for each goal, the criteria by which it's success will be measured. If your goal is to write a book in the coming year, does that mean the rough draft will be done, or does it mean that the manuscript will be in the publishers hands, or does it mean that the first run of 100,000 copies will be piled in the corner of your office? If your goal is to lose weight, lift weights, or simply throw your weight around, how much weight are we talking here?

TAKE ACTION!

If we never actually begin the journey, the whole process of mapping our destiny is an exercise in futility. Like Don the Dreamer, we will talk a good game but never have a chance to win. At some point, Moses had to leave Midian and get back to Egypt in order to lead God's people out of bondage.

> *"Thinking is easy, acting is difficult, and putting thoughts into action is the most difficult thing in the world."* (Johann von Goethe)

We aren't after perfection - only progress. As we explore our vision, ponder our purpose and identify our goals, exciting things begin to happen. God moves in supernatural ways, and our efforts begin to be multiplied many times over. Let's close this chapter as we began, by pursuing an encounter with the One who loves us and wants to lead us. Moses saw a burning bush, but God desires a burning heart. As Paul wrote in Ephesians, chapter three, He's waiting to take us far beyond what we could ever ask or think!

CHAPTER 6

Climbing Higher
The View is Incredible

"Tomorrow is a blank page."

For some, this statement is a relief. For others, it may breed anxiety. For still others, it is a concept which heightens the senses, gets the creative juices flowing, and just plain causes excitement!

Whatever our reaction, it is an indicator of what we are likely to write on our "page." The plain truth is, not one of us has passed this way before, and the only thing we can expect is the unexpected. Only God, in His omniscience and intentional will, knows what greatness or grief tomorrow may hold. As we have said, it is our reaction to tomorrow, not the events of it, which produce victory or defeat.

God, as is His nature, is calling us to new, bolder and higher places. He loves us far too much to allow us to remain as we are. He's *always* moving, always acting in our behalf, and He is quickening His pace. God is calling, preparing and releasing His people more rapidly than ever before. The Word of the Lord is being heard all over the world as "deep calls unto deep." Renewal, revival and harvest of souls is pervasive. No continent on earth is without tremendous exhibits of His hand at work. For the first time in all of history, the rate of salvations per capita is greater than the rate of deaths. What a privilege it is to live and serve the Lord "for such a time as this." What an opportunity we have before us in Word Wide Dream Builders as an organization.

What a shame it would be to one day realize that the "cloud" of God's directing, leading presence had long since left us behind, and we hadn't even known it was gone. Like Samson, we do what we have always done: *"And he awoke out of his sleep, and said, I will go out as at other times before... and he knew not that the LORD was departed from him"* (Judges 16:20). What does it take to ensure that we are following that cloud? How do we avoid the ditch of sameness that so easily deceives, convincing us that what was anointed yesterday still pulses with power today? How can we be assured that we are moving, not simply wandering?

As we desire to move with God, and to rise into new levels of relationship, service and leadership of people, we might see the task as a formidable mountain to climb. God is calling, "Come up higher," and we may be looking at the height of the mountain from "sea level," thinking we can never make it. Mountain climbers quickly learn that no summit is conquered all at once but rather in levels. Good mountain climbers plan (there's that word again) to scale a certain portion of the total elevation each day. As they reach each objective, they establish base camps. Climbing higher in purpose and destiny works much the same way.

Joshua, chosen to lead the Children of Israel to the promised land, knew that in order to live in a different land, they would need to learn to do different things and to do things differently. In Joshua chapter three, we see two essential character traits which are absolutely necessary to our ability to "go with God."

KEEP YOUR EYES ON THE ARK. (COMMITMENT)

> *"And it came to pass after three days, that the officers went through the host; And they commanded the people, saying, When ye see the Ark of the covenant of the LORD your God, and the priests the Levites bearing it, then ye shall remove from your place, and go*

*after it. Yet there shall be a space between
you and it, about two thousand cubits by
measure: come not near unto it, that ye may
know the way by which ye must go: for ye
have not passed this way heretofore."* (Joshua
3:2-4)

Two truths stand out in this passage.

■ When God moves, we move!

No hesitation, no questioning, no committees, no secret ballot
voting. It's simple really, isn't it? All it takes is commitment and
vigilance. Like troops on maneuvers, there are two requirements.

1. NEVER TAKE YOUR EYES OFF THE COMMANDER.

Joshua commanded the people, *"When you see the Ark . . . ."* The
people didn't know at what moment they would move, but they knew
where to look. A soldier's job is to stay alert and watch. We need to
be watchful in Spirit. Are our eyes on the presence of God (the Ark)?
If the presence of God in our lives (the Holy Spirit) begins to move,
would we know it?

2. BE PREPARED TO MOVE.

A good unit in the field of battle is *mobile*. They are free from
the things which would hinder immediate response to the command
to advance. *"For if after they have escaped the pollution of the world
through the knowledge of the Lord and Savior Jesus Christ, they are
again entangled therein, and overcome, the latter end is worse with
them than the beginning"* (2 Peter 2:20.) Jesus had strong words for
those who weren't prepared for immediate action.

"And another of his disciples said unto him,
Lord, suffer me first to go and bury my father.
But Jesus said unto him, Follow me; and let
the dead bury their dead."
(Matthew 8:21-22)

■   **Maintain perspective.**

The people were told to "keep a space" from the Ark. The sense here is that God wanted His people to follow Him, but He also wanted them to be aware of the land through which they would travel knowing the territory would serve them well in later battles with their enemies. God was taking them through places they had never been before (Joshua 3:4), and it was important that they pay attention! Is it possible to follow God *and* be aware of the world around us? Absolutely. It is this very knowledge of "the land" that will prepare us to fight effectively and occupy the territory. Every time God takes us somewhere new, we must have His perspective of the region.

PUT YOUR FEET IN THE WATER (COURAGE)

"And it shall come to pass, as soon as the soles
of the feet of the priests that bear the ark of
the LORD, the Lord of all the earth, shall rest
in the waters of Jordan, that the waters of
Jordan shall be cut off from the waters that
come down from above; and they shall stand
upon an heap. And as they that bare the ark
were come unto Jordan, and the feet of the
priests that bare the ark were dipped in the
brim of the water, (for Jordan overfloweth
all his banks all the time of harvest,) that the
waters which came down from above stood

*and rose up upon an heap very far from
the city Adam, that is beside Zaretan: and
those that came down toward the sea of the
plain, even the salt sea, failed, and were cut
off: and the people passed over right against
Jericho."* (Joshua 3:13, 15-16)

Is it possible to have commitment without courage? Well, yes and no. To what are we committed? If we are committed to church as usual and programs devoid of life, then our commitment may be great but very little courage is required. If, however, we are committed to a God of purpose and destiny who is intent on the ultimate defeat of the Enemy and the salvation of the world, courage is essential.

The Levites carrying the Ark were required to walk into the Jordan River at flood stage. Then, and only then, did something supernatural occur. Many today are crying out to God for a way to get to the promised land. Courage requires tremendous, even dangerous steps of faith. To go where He is leading, it is necessary to cross against the flood. Public opinion, personal doubt, and past mistakes may swell up around our feet, but the Word of God to His men and women of destiny is that we will walk across on dry ground! If we will act *before* we see it, we will see it. Take courage!

LET GO OF THE PAST

*"Remember ye not the former things, neither
consider the things of old."* (Isaiah 43:18)

Can we ever get to the place where we will be able to say that there are things in our past which were not good, but no matter how hard we try, we just can't seem to recall them? Notwithstanding, a disease or injury that affects our mental capacity, we probably won't forget. There is no "erase" button behind our left ear. We can't hit the "delete" key. How can we *remember not the former things?*" Paul said, *"...but this one thing I do, forgetting those things which are behind . . ."* (Philippians 3:13)

What these verses *don't* mean is that being really spiritual furnishes us with a convenient lapse of memory concerning those things which are not of God. In a court of law, when a judge asks the jury to disregard a comment from a witness or an attorney, can that jury forget what was just said? No! What the judge is asking of that jury is that those specific words not *influence* their judgement in the case. Practically, that is easier said than done. With the enemy whispering in our ear, it is a difficult thing not to be aware of our past as we try to move forward in the things of the Lord.

Past failure is the number one hindrance to our present and future success. Learning to *disregard* the past - not let it influence our present judgement - is essential to climbing higher. It's hard to move forward with God while dragging the baggage of the past. Whatever it was, whatever we've done or whatever was done to us, it's time to let the blood of the Cross wash it away in the total forgiveness of Christ. The grace of God is sufficient. His love for you is enough. Don't believe the lie that you are beyond His mercy. Let go of the past today.

Some people like to drag around their baggage like a dead cat! "Poor me," they say, "I have this dead cat." Then, as if that's not enough, they want *you* to *pet* it! "Please come pet my dead cat," as if to invoke our sympathy for their plight. Oddly enough, in the name of ministering to such folk, some will commiserate. "Oh, you poor dear. Your kitty's dead. How awful you must feel. How long has it been dead? Twenty years? Bless your heart!" Please don't misunderstand. Recent injuries must be treated with care and love. Time must be allowed for recovery. Eventually, though, we must move on. The past must be just that — the past. It's time to bury what's dead and quit dragging it around.

EMBRACE CHANGE

> *"Behold, I will do a new thing; now it shall spring forth; shall ye not know it? I will even make a way in the wilderness, and rivers in the desert."* (Isaiah. 43:19)

> *"... reaching forth unto those things which are before, I press toward the mark for the prize of the high calling of God in Christ Jesus."* (Philippians 4:13-14)

Change is here to stay. The only consistent thing in our lives is change. The Children of Israel, as Joshua led them into the promise land, were about to face the biggest changes of their lives. As God leads you and me into our purpose and destiny, there must be change. "But God never changes," you say. "He is the same yesterday, today and tomorrow." Yes, that's true. Concerning His nature, His forgiveness and His promises, He does not renege. His gifts and calling are without repentance. Praise be to God! However, His consistent, progressive revelation of His will, His purpose and His love for His people *will* produce change in us - every time. In fact, He loves us far too much to allow us to remain as we are. His desire for us to be more than sinners condemned to death moved Him to provide His Son as a sacrifice to *change* us into His children. Does His desire for us to change end there? Not hardly. *"But we all, with open face beholding as in a glass the glory of the Lord, are changed into the same image from glory to glory, even as by the Spirit of the Lord."* (2 Corinthians 3:18)

Embrace change. It's a good thing. It's a *God* thing.

EAGLES OR CHICKENS?

> *"As an eagle stirreth up her nest, fluttereth*
> *over her young, spreadeth abroad her wings,*
> *taketh them, beareth them on her wings."*
> (Deuteronomy 32:11)

Eagles are majestic looking birds as they soar high above the earth riding on the thermal currents with hardly a movement of wings. They speak to us of freedom, courage and sufficiency. They live with almost no predatory risk, high above the reach of the petty thieves which would steal their eggs or harm their young. Sounds good, doesn't it?

God chose this analogy in Deuteronomy, purposefully. He wants to convey something to His people. We are to live like eagles! The present reality is, many of us don't. You know the comparison: Eagles cannot be happy scratching around in the barnyard. They have to be free to soar. They live in high elevations.

God had already given the Children of Israel the "eagle treatment." *"Ye have seen what I did unto the Egyptians, and how I bare you on eagles' wings, and brought you unto myself."* (Exodus 19:4)

Eagles are protective of their young, but they know that in order to survive, they have to learn to fly on their own. Let's look at the process:

■ *Stirs up its nest*

When it's time for the young eagle to leave the nest, the mother eagle has a way of making the nest uncomfortable. What has been a place of nurturing and safety begins to change (there's that word again). The mother eagle actually begins to tear at the fabric of the nest. The young birds begin to sense the instability. To the immature eagle, there is an immediate sense of danger. The young may even believe an enemy is at work. Even eagle parents seem to sense the truth that change occurs only when the pain of staying the same is greater than the pain of the change itself. Is your "nest" being disturbed? God is a far better parent than an eagle. He loves us too much to allow us to remain in the nest too long.

■   *Fluttereth over her young*

If the young eagles don't take the hint when the nest is torn, mother eagle begins step two. She starts to beat her wings over her young. The same wings which days before were spread over them in cover, warmth and safety have now become the source of real motivation! The nest is torn, there is commotion in the air, and the young eagle has never been more insecure. He is chased to the very edge of the nest.

■   *Carrying them on its wings*

Out into the unknown goes the eaglet, knowing only that he couldn't remain where he was any longer; wondering if the one who had given him life and kept him safe had totally abandoned him. Trying to fly, there is a tentative flap of wings - then a furious burst of energy - neither of which have the desired effect. He is falling. Awaiting the impact of the ground, he suddenly feels himself rising again! He's being carried! Yes! What a ride! Higher even than the height of the nest he is carried. Higher than he's ever been before, and then . . . he is out on his own again, falling, flailing, but not quite as quickly. An eagle is learning to fly.

What about the eagle that refuses to fly on its own? What happens when creation purpose goes unfulfilled? Life on the ground is very, very different. For the chicken, the barnyard is all they know. For the eagle who winds up there, it's a place of frustrating, unfulfilled destiny.

> *"O Jerusalem, Jerusalem, thou that killest the*
> *prophets, and stonest them which are sent*
> *unto thee, how often would I have gathered*
> *thy children together, even as a hen gathereth*
> *her chickens under her wings, and ye would*
> *not!"* (Matthew 23:37)

Jesus says in this passage that there are those who should be soaring like eagles who live like chickens. In fact, they're not even very good chickens, for they don't even know how to find their place under His wings. The call goes out to the young, but they are scattered and scurrying around the barnyard. What's it like in the barnyard? What is it like in a man-created religious system which refuses to allow us to be the eagles we are created to be?

■ It's confining.

There are limitations called fences around the barnyard. Freedom is a foreign concept. The world, according to chickens, is a very small place. The only thing worse than living in confinement is living in confinement and not knowing it. The barnyard is a place of bondage.

■ It's boring.

There's not much happening in the barnyard that is new, fresh or exciting. The territory is familiar. The routine is familiar. The air is not fresh. In the barnyard, the faces stay basically the same, day to day. A few die, and a few are born, but the number of residents never significantly changes. Why would it? Who would want to invite anyone to a barnyard? Who would want to come? Nothing much ever changes in the barnyard.

> Two deacons were participating in a
> new program sponsored by their church.
> As they stood on the porch of a home,
> waiting for a response to the doorbell, one
> commented, "I really like this new 'outreach'
> thing we're doing now." "Yeah, me too,"
> replied the other. "But it's sure a lot like
> 'visitation', isn't it?"

■ **It's insecure.**

Anything new or unknown brings immediate fear to the barnyard. The first hint of a storm sends it's residents running for cover. Cowering in fear, chickens become agitated, remaining upset long after the threat has passed. Eagles, however, approach storm clouds differently. Rising in the air, they allow the quickening winds to lift them higher and higher until suddenly they find themselves *above* the storm with a unique perspective of it's direction and strength. A common response, even among believers, to the greeting, "How are you?" is, "Pretty well, under the circumstances." Eagles don't live *under* the circumstances. The barnyard is a place of fear.

■ **It's conforming.**

Chickens run in bunches. As they scurry around their dreary territory, they move together like they have strings attached. When one changes direction, they all change. If one gets separated, it quickly returns to the bunch. Chickens are not great individualists. They have a crowd mentality, and the crowd rarely does the right thing. Eagles move at the influence of the wind. It is their buoyancy, and it is their barometer. There are no unique, personal destinies in the barnyard. Chickens flock together. Eagle sore alone but are not loners.

■ **It's filthy.**

Chickens will eat almost anything on the ground. They are not discriminating eaters. Husks, hulls, garbage, litter, as well as grains will do for a chicken. The ground in the barnyard is bare; The chickens have either eaten it or scratched it away. Barnyard mentalities cause us to "take in" just about anything. Verbal trash, rumor and rotten communication fills the belly of the barnyard believer, and when new garbage is found, there is ample "clucking" to alert the others to join in. The barnyard is a nasty place.

Eagles have tremendous vision.

> *"Doth the eagle mount up at thy command,
> and make her nest on high? She dwelleth
> and abideth on the rock, upon the crag of the
> rock, and the strong place. From thence she
> seeketh the prey, and her eyes behold afar off."*
> (Job 39:27-29)

And they are fast.

> *". . . as swift as the eagle flieth;"*
> (Deuteronomy 28:49)

It takes the supernatural to change the nature of something. Man can dress it up, disguise it, and even re-name it, but only God can change it's nature. The word defines itself. Super (above, transcendent) natural (normal, expected). God is a *supernatural* God. He is about changing the nature of things. The same God which changed us from condemned to redeemed can change us from chickens to eagles in *nature*. We can't just begin to soar on our own. We must *receive* the nature of an eagle from Him. Ask God to place this spirit—His Spirit —within you; then receive it as a gift.

THE COST OF CLIMBING HIGHER

Ralph Waldo Emerson said, "For everything gained, something is lost." Every breakthrough is also a "break with." Jesus told His disciples that a wise man assesses his resources before beginning a task:

> *"For which of you, intending to build a tower,*
> *sitteth not down first, and counteth the cost,*
> *whether he have sufficient to finish it? Lest*
> *haply, after he hath laid the foundation,*
> *and is not able to finish it, all that behold it*
> *begin to mock him, Saying, This man began*
> *to build, and was not able to finish. Or what*
> *king, going to make war against another*
> *king, sitteth not down first, and consulteth*
> *whether he be able with ten thousand to meet*
> *him that cometh against him with twenty*
> *thousand?"* (Luke 14:28-31)

There is a cost to climbing higher. There are sacrifices to be made. Choices between our own desires and that which will move us toward our goal must become second nature. One of the stumbling blocks to success is that we have not learned to differentiate between price and cost. If we buy a pair of shoes that have a low price tag, but only last a year and are worn out, the actual cost is greater than if we bought a pair priced twice as much but lasting five to ten years time. Most of us are looking for the lowest price instead of truly counting the cost. Consequently, most merchandise in America is made to be disposable —and cheap. Craftsmanship and quality are rare.

Unfortunately, this mind set has affected our sense of destiny as well. Many saints are willing to settle for the inexpensive and transient rather than the valuable and lasting. Don't be deceived by that which appears to be gold but isn't. Making a Kingdom difference in the world is costly. Only a few are willing to pay the price.

> "You pay a price for getting stronger. You pay a price for getting faster. You pay a price for jumping higher, but you also pay a price for staying the same." *(H. Jackson Brown, Life's Little Instruction Book)*

IN ORDER TO CLIMB HIGHER WITH GOD, WE MUST BE WILLING TO CHOOSE:
■ **The approval of God over the praise of men.**

The Apostle Paul was a man who had earned the right to be admired by the people of his day. His education, his zeal and the recognition of his peers was as good as it gets. He was on his way to being one of the great men of his time in the eyes of all who knew him. *"Though I might also have confidence in the flesh. If any other man thinketh that he hath whereof he might trust in the flesh, I more..."* (Philippians 3:4) He came to realize, though, that there was a greater approval than that of his fellow man. *"But what things were gain to me, those I counted loss for Christ. Yea doubtless, and I count all things but loss for the excellency of the knowledge of Christ Jesus my Lord: for whom I have suffered the loss of all things, and do count them but dung, that I may win Christ."* (Philippians 3:7-8)

There is an interesting story told by the gatherers of a great sea food delicacy, the blue crab. It seems that, when gathering these creatures into buckets, one need only be concerned that the first one escape. When the second (and any after) is added to the container, any crab endeavoring to climb out is immediately grabbed by his fellow prisoners and prohibited from attaining freedom! The praise of man will invariably keep us from reaching God's highest call.

■ **Excellence over average.** *"Whatsoever thy hand findeth to do, do it with thy might."* **(Ecclesiastes 9:10)**

> "Mediocrity is a region bounded on the
> north by compromise, on the south by
> indecision, on the east by past thinking, and
> the west by a lack of vision." (John Mason,
> *An Enemy called Average)*

Excellence is always a choice. Excellence (or the lack thereof) is not an indicator of talent, personality or gifting. In fact, the more gifted or talented the person, the more likelihood of their allowing that ability to get them through the task without the need or desire to work hard and do their best.

Daniel 6:3-4 describes the characteristics of an excellent spirit:

> "Then this Daniel was preferred above the
> presidents and princes, because an excellent
> spirit was in him; and the king thought
> to set him over the whole realm. Then
> the presidents and princes sought to find
> occasion against Daniel concerning the

kingdom; but they could find none occasion
nor fault; forasmuch as he was faithful,
neither was there any error or fault found in
him."

According to verse three, Daniel had a spirit of excellence or an
excellent spirit. In verse four, we are told that he was *faultless*. We are
not to believe that he was sinless, but that when his jealous enemies
tried to find the "dirt" on him, they came up empty handed. They
could find no charge against him *concerning the kingdom*. What a
testimony! There was no *error* in him. This doesn't mean he never
made a mistake. The word here has the sense of something constructed
so as to be perfectly fitted together. Every part is exactly the size and
shape it should be in order to make the whole thing symmetrical.
Daniel was completely "lined up" with those he was serving. No one
could find anything out of place.

Not only was he faultless, he was *faithful*. In other words, he was
obedient to those in authority over him. The missing trait of excellence
today is that of submission to authority. The spirit of rebellion
is rampant. Authority, due to its misuse by a few, is mistrusted,
lambasted and scorned. Loyalty, devotion and dedication are qualities
rarely seen in the workplace. Sadly, it is missing in the church, as well.
An excellent spirit is one that produces long-term relationships. I
believe one of the reasons there are so many "spiritual gypsies" among
believers today is that pastors and church leaders move around more
than the people! The average tenure of pastors in denominational
churches in America is around two and a half years! Of course, just
staying a long time in one place does not define faithfulness, but it's a
great start. Faithfulness is both staying and serving. The parable of
the talents illustrates that faithfulness to serve someone else's work is
prerequisite to having our own. (Matthew.25:14) Settling for average
results will exclude us from climbing higher.

■ **Destiny over dollar signs.**
The word of God is clear: We cannot serve God and materialism.
A man named Simon learned this lesson the hard way.

> *"And when Simon saw that through laying*
> *on of the apostles' hands the Holy Ghost was*
> *given, he offered them money, saying, 'Give*
> *me also this power, that on whomsoever I*
> *lay hands, he may receive the Holy Ghost.'*
> *But Peter said unto him, 'Thy money perish*
> *with thee, because thou hast thought that the*
> *gift of God may be purchased with money.'"*
> (Acts. 8:18-19)

Many people with tremendous potential for the Kingdom are living in misery today due to decisions made in favor of dollars rather than destiny. Simon isn't the only biblical character who let money prevent him from great destiny in Christ. Judas betrayed Jesus, and was paid in silver. He took his own life in the agony of remorse and guilt. (Acts 1:8) Ananias and Sapphira lied to the church leaders and to God concerning the price of a piece of land. They left the church horizontally. (Acts 5:1) It seems that God takes this business of putting things ahead of Him seriously! More is said in scripture about money than about many other things we think are much more important. The bible says a lot about money. Unfortunately, the church says very little about it. As a result, the United States is a nation which votes with it's pocket book. The last two national elections have been about a good economy instead of about character, integrity and spiritual values. We have said to our politicians that, as long as interest rates and unemployment are low, we don't really care if they are truthful, ethical or moral. God will not hold us guiltless as a nation for the choices we have made. We have valued a quick dollar and expediency over the hard choices to do the right thing.

Money is amoral. It has no sense of right or wrong. I read several years ago of a struggling single Mom who held the winning ticket to a multi-million dollar lottery. On the advice of her pastor, who said God would not bless her because the money came from gambling, she destroyed the ticket! Incredible! If a Columbian drug lord walked in to our office and offered us a great sum of money, we'd take it so fast you couldn't watch it happen. Then we'd cast the demons out of it and use it for the glory of God. We'd thank God for His provision (there are many examples in scripture of God's work being financed by unbelievers), and we'd use that money in a heart beat. Now, if there were any strings attached or pressure brought to bear about how the money should be used, or favors that might be requested — NO WAY!

Money is nothing more than a tool, and tools can be used for good or evil. The *love* of money is the root of all evil. I hear people make promises about what they would do for the church if they "struck it rich." The truth is, they wouldn't do any more if they were rich than they are doing now - maybe less. If we are generous now, we'll be generous with more. If we are stingy now, we'd just be rich and stingy if we had a lot of money. More money only magnifies what's already in our hearts. It's not money that's the root of all evil, it's to love it and serve it more than to love and serve God that's the root of all evil.

■ **What's best over what's good.**

We are all bombarded daily by things that clutch at our time and attention, and most of these are good things. This committee, that service club, this bible study or that community project are pitched to us as if their very survival depends upon our involvement. We find ourselves over booked, over committed, under rested and under pressure. We begin to neglect details and find ourselves "skimming" through the day in crisis mode going ninety miles per hour with our hair on fire. The most important things in our lives are neglected. The worst enemy of that which is best is that which is good. Paul said that he had committed himself to focus on the best. *". . . but this one thing I do . . ."* (Philippians 3:13) What is your "one thing?" What is your highest and best calling? Climbing higher means focusing on the objective. Earl Nightengale said, "Studying one subject one hour a day for five years will make you one of the foremost authorities in the *world* on that subject." Staying with the best is essential to reaching higher in the Spirit.

■ **Significance over security.**

Tom Brokaw, noted television news anchorman, says, "It's easy to make a buck. It's a lot tougher to make a difference." Security is a natural desire. We all need to feel safe physically, emotionally, relationally and spiritually. Studies have shown that insecurity can lead to mental, emotional and even physical dysfunction. Insecure people have shorter life expectancies and more health problems. God's very nature and plan is designed to bring His children into a place of assurance and confidence through a right relationship with Him. He is very determined, however, that our security is in Him and Him alone. He will see to it that our false feelings of security and safety are consistently eliminated until we have only His provision left to trust. In order to reach new levels of Kingdom purpose, we will most certainly have to trade our own sense of security for significance in Him. We read in Acts 21:10-14 that Paul faced a choice between his own personal safety and the calling of the Spirit to go to Jerusalem. Even a noted prophet urged him not to go, saying that the Holy Spirit had shown him the danger for Paul.

*"Then Paul answered, 'What mean ye to
weep and to break mine heart? For I am
ready not to be bound only, but also to die
at Jerusalem for the name of the Lord Jesus.'
And when he would not be persuaded, we
ceased, saying, 'The will of the Lord be done.'"*
(Acts 21:13-14)

If God is calling us to new levels of significance and service, and
we truly desire to reach our destiny potential, it is imperative that we
identify and deal with the things that "hinder" the process. What false
security blankets, like Linus of *Peanuts* cartoon fame, are we holding
too tightly? Ask the Holy Spirit to reveal them right now. Take a
moment from this book and settle the issues permanently. God is our
singular certainty, our only confidence, our sole assurance. Climbing
higher means taking risks that only God can see us through.

THE SECRET TO CLIMBING HIGHER

Standing at the crossroads of decision concerning new levels
of destiny and purpose, we have choices to make. We can choose
to get what's easy to obtain and miss or delay God's best for us; We
can choose to stay where we are, which is actually a choice to miss
out completely, or we can choose to leave behind anything that keeps
us from reaching new levels of significance in Him in order to make
first things truly first. Would we trade an older model, badly running
automobile for this year's newest, most efficient sports car? Will we
"trade up" with God giving Him our old attitudes in return for a
renewed mind that allows us to reach new heights of spiritual success?

The two keys are sacrifice and persistence. Make wise choices
and keep trying. It's that simple. There are no excuses in the minds
of those who accomplish much for God. There is no "If only," and

no "I can't." There is a continual perseverance to develop character that will withstand the tests and temptations of the Enemy. There is a constant hunger for the privilege of a higher calling and greater place of service, and there is a practiced and persistent self discipline which prepares us to finish well what God has called us to do.

Someone has said that both fools and the wise do the same things; The wise simply do them much sooner. E.M. Gray said, "The successful person does by habit the things failures don't like to do." I want to do the things God has called me to do. I want to do them now, and I want to do them well.

Years ago, two French climbers were caught in a sudden snow blizzard while climbing K-2. They knew that to settle in until the blizzard passed would be certain death, and they were too near the top to go back. They had but one choice: Climb, climb, climb and try to get above the storm.

They were unsuccessful in their attempt.

Years later, the family had some fellow climbers and friend traverse K-2 and place a plaque approximately where they perished. For anyone who passed that way, it was a memorial and a testimony of their bravery and tenacity. The plaque had their names engraved with the date they perished that simply said, "They died climbing."

Climb, dear friend, and let those words be your epitaph.

CHAPTER 7

A Life of Integrity
An Inside Job

Integrity: (n) 1. Soundness; 2. Adherence to
a code of moral, artistic or spiritual values;
3. The quality or state of being complete or
undivided; completeness.

We live in a cynical society.

We have learned the hard way to be wary, suspicious and on our guard around most people. We trust very little, and we trust very few. We are skeptical, doubtful, leery and apprehensive when asked to reveal personal or private information. We have been burned, and as the proverb goes, "He who sits on a hot stove will not sit on any stove for a long, long time." Businessmen and preachers alike are subject to being viewed through a filter in which a few scurrilous elements have been portrayed as true cross-sections of their professions.

I recently spoke with an airline pilot who was extremely negative about pastors. He didn't go to church, it seems, because he had seen one or two television preachers admit to doing wrong. My reply was this, "I recently heard of a pilot who was removed from his position because he had reported to work with a rather elevated blood alcohol level, but that doesn't keep me from flying!" In our current society, we must overcome perception with extraordinary lifestyles. Isn't that the standard God expects, anyway?

> *"If so be that ye have heard him, and have
> been taught by him, as the truth is in Jesus:*

> *That ye put off concerning the former*
> *conversation the old man, which is corrupt*
> *according to the deceitful lusts; And be*
> *renewed in the spirit of your mind; And that*
> *ye put on the new man, which after God is*
> *created in righteousness and true holiness."*
> (Ephesians 4:21-24)

Integrity is often summarized as "walking the talk." It has also been defined as, "What we do when we know no one is watching." Socrates said, "The first key to greatness is to be in reality what we appear to be." Let's look at ten truths about integrity.

■ Integrity is a choice.

Just as the attitude we have is the result of a choice we make, integrity requires us to be proactive. Living our lives true to our word and full of character is not something that just sort of happens. But, on the other hand, it's more than a proclamation. As a matter of fact, anyone who constantly talks about their high standards of integrity is most likely trying to convince themselves! Like humility, integrity is a quality in us that is recognized by others. Bragging about it means, "You ain't got it!"

> *"Let your heart therefore be perfect with the*
> *LORD our God, to walk in his statutes, and*
> *to keep his commandments, as at this day."*
> (1 Kings 8:61)

■ Integrity is important to God.

Unfortunately, His people often fall far short of God's standards. He has promises for each eventuality.

> *"And if thou wilt walk before me, as David*

> *thy father walked, in integrity of heart, and*
> *in uprightness, to do according to all that*
> *I have commanded thee, and wilt keep my*
> *statutes and my judgments: Then I will*
> *establish the throne of thy kingdom upon*
> *Israel for ever, as I promised to David thy*
> *father, saying, There shall not fail thee a man*
> *upon the throne of Israel. But if ye shall at all*
> *turn from following me, ye or your children,*
> *and will not keep my commandments and*
> *my statutes which I have set before you, but*
> *go and serve other gods, and worship them:*
> *Then will I cut off Israel out of the land which*
> *I have given them; and this house, which I*
> *have hallowed for my name, will I cast out*
> *of my sight; and Israel shall be a proverb and*
> *a byword among all people . . . ."* (1 Kings
> 9:4-7)

■ **Integrity is more valuable than material wealth.**

The cemeteries of the earth are filled with those who thought character mattered less than money, and who found themselves so empty they took their own lives. Billions of dollars cannot make up for the inability to look at the reflection in the mirror.

> *"Better is the poor that walketh in his*
> *uprightness, than he that is perverse in his*
> *ways, though he be rich."* (Proverbs 28:6)

■ **Integrity pleases God.**

The heart of every good father rejoices in every indication that his son is showing characteristics similar to his own. How much more, then, does the heart of our Father God delight in His children whose character imitates His own! God, you see, is integrity to the "nth" degree. His promises are "yea and amen." His gifts and callings are without repentance. He is the same yesterday, today and tomorrow. His Word never fails! To be men and women of integrity is to be like God!

> *"I know, my God, that you test the heart and are pleased with integrity."* (1 Chronicles 29:17 - NKJ)

■ **Integrity means no hypocrisy.**

Two elderly ladies were finishing their visit to the cemetery plot of a recently deceased loved one. As they made their way back to their automobile, they paused to read the epitaph on a particular marker. "Here lies a politician and an honest man." One turned to the other and exclaimed, "Imagine that, they're putting two bodies in one grave these days!" As we have said earlier, integrity means we do what we say and say what we do.

■ **Integrity is a matter of the heart.**

Lack of integrity destroys everything around us, but ultimately it kills us from the inside out. The worst consequence of living without integrity is that we begin to despise *ourselves*. Leadership requires asking people to follow us, and we won't be very convincing if, at the core of our souls, we don't think we're worth following. Inner discontentment shows. People pick up on it. Integrity is like our own personal inner glue. It holds us together when everything around us is crumbling and no one is standing at our side. The only way to get through the times when we are called upon to stand against the crowd is to be able to say before ourselves and before God, "I did the right thing."

■ **Integrity is lived, not "lipped."**

"Do what I say, not what I do," is the motto of many high profile people these days. Charles Barkley, professional basketball player, once railed at the notion that he had a great responsibility to be a role model for children. "I'm not a role model! I don't want to be a role model!," he screamed. Well, the latter may be true, but the former is a pipe dream. *Every* adult is a role model for some child. The higher the visibility, the greater the responsibility.

We are told by those who study such things that what we learn is ten percent auditory, eighty-nine percent visual, and only one percent through other senses. It stands to reason that people follow those who tell them and then show them. What they hear, they *understand*; what they see, they *believe*.

■ **Integrity is reality, not image.**

One of the highest paid occupations in government these days is that of being an image consultant. Countless hours and many millions of dollars are spent attempting to put just the right "face" on a situation or event. "Make me look good," is the challenge thrown at speech writers, wardrobe consultants, makeup artists and personal advisors. Generations of television watchers have necessitated the dependency of elected officials on Hollywood more than their own values and ethics. "Smoke and mirrors" are the tools of successful politicians. As Robert Deniro's character in *Wag the Dog* said, "The public will believe what we tell them to believe." God says, however, that integrity is an inside job.

> *"Behold, thou desirest truth in the inward
> parts."* (Psalms 51:6)

■ **Integrity is first personal, then public.**

Stephen R. Covey, of the *Covey Leadership Center* says, "Private victory always precedes public victory." Integrity in our relationships, our professional lives and our arena of influence is only as good as our internal character. A refusal to be honest with ourselves guarantees our inability to deal truthfully with others.

> *"For as he thinketh in his heart, so is he."*
> (Proverbs 23:7)

■ **Integrity opposes the spirit of our age.**

We live under the influence of a spirit of situational ethics. Whether a thing is righteous or true depends upon prevailing circumstances. Politicians don't lie, they provide disinformation. Stealing is alright if you take from someone who has more than enough. Sex outside of marriage is acceptable, if there is at least some sense of commitment. Our children aren't wrong to disobey parents, teachers and law enforcement officials, because they are victims of "the system." I read the story of a woman who happened to be nearby when an armored car overturned and spilled thousands of dollars into the street. She was quoted as saying, "Praise God! He has met my need," as she stuffed all she could grab into her purse, clothes and even her shoes! An honest person who returns a lost wallet with cash intact is regarded as foolish. It's a battle to maintain integrity in our day.

THE BURDEN OF INTEGRITY

Personal integrity is not determined by environment. Many "experts" are advocating a removal of responsibility and culpability for law breaking today saying that family and/or society is to blame for individual acts of evil. While it is true that the erosion of the traditional family unit has resulted in a rise in juvenile crime, the results of this crime is a reality. Its victims still suffer, and its penalties should still be enforced. Children who are old enough to steal, assault or kill are old enough to know what's right and what's wrong. It's all about choices. How can two people grow up in the same household, one becoming a productive, responsible citizen, the other stays in and out of jail for petty theft? Choices. Our circumstances are responsible for our actions in the same way a mirror is responsible for how we look. Our actions are simply reflections of who we are.

Integrity is not a function of achievement. Great things have been accomplished by men and women who were woefully lacking in character and integrity. Notoriety, position, title, rank and influence are often more an indication of a lack rather than an abundance of decency and virtue. At the end of the day, all accomplishment not anchored in and bounded by a strong sense of values and principles will result in self destruction. The very attainments for which ones standards have been sacrificed become an epitaph.

Years ago, craftsmen and artisans placed a mark on their work to identify its creator. This mark was known as their character. A friend of mine was traveling in England some years ago, and was taken by his driver on a side trip to see some thatched-roofed houses constructed centuries before. On the end of the gable, woven into the thatch, was the craftsman's character, a duck. The driver pointed out that this symbol would unmistakably identify the workman. What would happen today if suddenly we were all required to identify our "work" with our individual character?

Integrity is not what others perceive us to be. Reputation is the result of character, not the cause of it. A good reputation is invaluable. D.L. Moody wrote, "If I take care of my character, my reputation will take care of itself." Reputation is what you have when you come into new relationships. Character is what you have when you go away. Reputation is made in a moment. Character is built over a lifetime. Reputation is what is written on your tombstone. Character is what angels testify about you at the throne of God!

> *"A good name is rather to be chosen than*
> *great riches, and loving favour rather than*
> *silver and gold."* (Proverbs 22:1)
> *"A good name is better than precious*
> *ointment."* (Ecclesiastes 7:1)

Integrity is not environment, achievement or reputation. It can, and should be, however, our best friend. A lifestyle of integrity will never betray us. It keeps our priorities clear, and it never allows us to be found in compromising situations. Abraham Lincoln once said, "When I lay down the reins of this administration, I want to be sure I have one friend left, and that is the friend inside myself." Thomas Jefferson offered this prayer: "God grant that men of principle shall be our principle men."

Take the Integrity Test
(from *Becoming a Person of Influence*, by Jim Dornan)

1.   HOW WELL DO I TREAT PEOPLE FROM WHOM I CAN GAIN NOTHING?
2.   AM I TRANSPARENT WITH OTHERS?
3.   DO I ROLE-PLAY BASED ON THE PERSON I'M WITH?

4. **AM I THE SAME PERSON IN THE SPOTLIGHT THAT I AM WHEN I'M ALONE?**

5. **DO I QUICKLY ADMIT WRONG DOING WITHOUT BEING PRESSED TO DO SO?**

6. **DO I PUT OTHERS AHEAD OF MY OWN AGENDA?**

7. **DO I HAVE UNCHANGING STANDARDS FOR MORAL DECISIONS, OR DO CIRCUMSTANCES DICTATE MY CHOICES?**

8. **AM I ACCOUNTABLE TO AT LEAST ONE OTHER PERSON FOR WHAT I THINK, SAY AND DO?**

9. **DO I MAKE DIFFICULT CHOICES, EVEN WHEN THEY HAVE PERSONAL COST ATTACHED?**

THE BENEFITS OF INTEGRITY

If integrity is hard to build, easy to lose and difficult to maintain, why bother? Why not, as our teen generation would say, "just slide?" Why do things the hard way, even when no one will ever know the difference? Integrity is not just a set of rules in God's training manual designed to see if we can measure up. Integrity is a necessary ingredient in building a life of confidence and steadfastness upon which God can place the weight of leadership. Let me suggest several benefits.

➤ **Integrity builds trust.**

Former President Dwight D. Eisenhower said, "In order to be a leader a man must have followers, and to have followers a man must have their confidence. Hence, the supreme quality for a leader is unquestionably integrity. Without it, no real success is possible. His teachings must square with his actions. The first great need, therefore, is integrity and high purpose." Its value to leadership aside, trust is a necessary ingredient to all relationships. Our need to trust and be trusted is integral to our creation purpose, and our ability to trust is a function of our own trustworthiness.

➤ **Integrity determines influence.**

"Every great institution is the lengthened shadow of a single man. His character determines the character of the organization." (Ralph Waldo Emerson) Will Rogers said, "People's minds are changed through observation, not argument." People without integrity will influence people without integrity. Associations built around anything less than principles and character will amount to nothing less than a band of thieves and crooks. It's ludicrous to believe that unprincipled people will honor their leaders. Integrity, on the other hand, attracts integrity.

➤ **Integrity means lasting commitments.**

Every great leader wants to build something that will remain long after he or she is gone from the scene. Consistent, intentional treatment of those who follow produces dedicated, steadfast disciples. People may be attracted to our vision, but they will stay because of *our* commitment to *them*.

➤ **Integrity fosters personal growth.**

Leaders must constantly grow in order to stay in the lead. It is impossible to lead others where we haven't been ourselves! We may fool a few people for a while, but eventually our stagnation will become evident. Jim Rohn in *The Treasury of Quotes*, says, "The value of accomplishment is not in what we obtain, but in what we become."

➤ **Integrity produces confidence.**

The ability to live consistently within the biblical directives of honesty, trustworthiness and righteousness is a victory upon which further battles can be fought with assurance. Self-discipline, inner peace and determination result. The man or woman who has conquered their own soul is a force with which the Enemy must reckon. Certainly, our strength is in Christ and Christ alone, but it is "Christ in us - the hope of glory." (Colossians 1:27)

> Billy Graham said, *"Integrity is the glue*
> *that holds our way of life together. We must*
> *constantly strive to keep our integrity intact."*

When wealth is lost, nothing is lost. When health is lost, something is lost. When character is lost, *all* is lost.

> *"Whoso offereth praise glorifieth me: and to*
> *him that ordereth his (lifestyle) aright will I*
> *show the salvation of God."* (Psalms 50:23)

CHAPTER 8

Dealing with Destiny's Detours
Don't Fret — Redirect

> *detour:* (n) 1. a deviation from a direct
> course or the usual procedure; a roundabout
> way temporarily replacing part of a route.

The purpose of a detour is not to keep us from our destination but to avoid trouble ahead.

We groan when we come upon a rerouted road. We know that we will have to take a route that, 1) is lesser, usually narrower and bumpier road, and 2) will almost certainly mean a longer, more time consuming trip. I've never traveled with anyone who unexpectedly came to a detour sign and said, "Praise God! A detour! Let's see where this will take us!" Detours are not happy occasions.

Do you know why the guys who hold the signs at highway construction sites hardly ever smile? They are responding to the reactions of the motorists passing by. Highway "sign guys" never hear a, "Thank you, we appreciate the hard work you do to improve the quality of our roadways." If they did, they'd drop their signs (and chins) in shock! We don't like detours. They interfere with our frantically paced, headlong rush to boredom and mediocrity.

REACTIONS TO DETOURS

There are varied reactions to unexpected detours (It is important to say *unexpected*. Detours we are aware of from the start don't bother us. We just travel them until the way is once again clear). These reactions can be due to anger, fear, frustration or impatience. Some people come to a detour sign and . . .

■ *Turn around.* The first sign that the trip is not going to go completely trouble free is all it takes to send some folk home. "I knew this wasn't a good idea," they say. "God is showing us we shouldn't have started. If this was God's will, we wouldn't be having this difficulty." I sure am glad Jesus didn't have that mind set as He faced the cross, aren't you?

■ *Blame others.* "Why didn't they warn us before we got here? If I'd known about this, I wouldn't have planned the trip in the first place. Couldn't they do this work another time?" Or, to listen to the more spiritual among us, "Well, I was willing, but no one would let me do things like God told me to do them. I could have been a blessing to many, if only *they* hadn't been in my way."

■ *Stop there.* Without ever having been somewhere, we could be easily fooled into thinking, "This is it." Because we are at the (temporary) end of this particular highway, we can go no further. We may look at the detour and say that because it is heading in a different direction, it can't be the correct way. Many people called to ministry have stopped far short of destiny simply because they accepted a temporary detour as the end of the line.

■ *Look for their own alternative.* Some people can never seem to accept direction. There is an inner drive to go their own way. "This detour will take far too long," they say, and immediately take off in another direction. Remember the Lord's word to Joshua to follow the Ark while observing the route? "For you have not passed this way before." (Joshua 3:4) When on a journey into unfamiliar territory, it's best to follow the signs. Those who have gone before us should be heeded with great care. It's also important to have an accurate map (remember 'Mapping your Destiny'?). Your leaders (up line) are in your life for a reason. Allow them to help guide you through challenges they've already been through.

■ *Ignore the signs.* The fallacy of this reaction is obvious. Trouble! Danger! Hazard! People who insist on ignoring the warning signals of impending danger should see one more sign just before the wreck happens; "See there, Dummy!" You've heard Jeff Foxworthy's line: "What's the last thing a Red-neck ever says?" "Hey, y'all, watch this!" Detours exist for a reason. Don't find out the hard way. It's not necessary, and it's much more painful.

Just as the most detailed and current map cannot be expected to show every detour, bypass or diversion we might face, the best laid plans of pursuing God's best for our lives will have side trips and deviations. Any of the reactions listed above will allow those detours to delay or even abort our destinies.

It is important to realize that detours can either be self imposed or God ordained. Correctly identifying the source, and handling the process with character and endurance assures that lessons will be learned and that our destination is attained. How we handle the detours on our destiny highway determine how quickly we get to enjoy the fulness and joy of walking in God's complete purpose for our lives.

DEMONIC DELAY OR DIVINE DETOUR?

God's "side roads" may seem like the work of the Enemy, but, in fact, are actually His hand of preparation on our lives. His word tells us that we are to rejoice in tribulation (tests).

> *"In this you greatly rejoice, though now for a*
> *little while, if need be, you have been grieved*
> *by various trials, that the genuineness of your*
> *faith, being much more precious than gold*
> *that perishes, though it is tested by fire, may*
> *be found to praise, honor, and glory at the*
> *revelation of Jesus Christ . . . ."* (1 Peter 1:6-7)

How do we determine whether we are in a demonic delay or a divine detour? Let me suggest that our reaction to the situation may have a great deal to do with the answer. If, when we encounter the unexpected, we pout, quit, get mad at God and our family and friends, the Enemy is indeed involved and active. If, on the other hand, circumstances are seen as challenges to be overcome and opportunities for God to do miracles, we can be sure that He will get the glory. The account of the man blind from birth in John 9:1 and following indicates this truth. The prevailing attitude of the day, voiced by Jesus' disciples, was that sickness or disability was always the result of the work of the devil or the sin of the individual. Jesus, however, exploded their theology by revealing that the sole purpose of this man's lifetime of blindness was for that very moment's opportunity for God's glory! Let's examine some less-than-divine detours to destiny.

FALSE EXPECTATIONS

False expectations come from two sources:

1.) *Others*: Our parents may place an incredible burden on us to live up to the dreams they have for us. It may be that their dreams are shaped by what they wished to be themselves but never achieved, rather than from insight into the destiny that God designed for their child. Scripture admonishes us to, "Train up a child in the way he should go . . ." (Proverbs 22:6), not in the way we think they should go. Friends, employers, co-workers and family can be just as guilty. God is much better at determining a life's direction than anyone else I know! We must turn down the volume of what significant others are saying enough to clearly hear and follow God's voice.

2.) *Ourselves*: We may become our own worst enemy when it comes to finding and walking in our destiny. If we begin looking at the ways others are accomplishing great things in the Kingdom and try to be just like them, we can completely miss the unique destiny God has design just for us. Seeking for our destiny by watching what others are doing rather than by listening to God and mature Christians who can provide counsel and/or accountability can spell disaster. Without the proper direction we may wind up living with great frustration and anxiety, because we are unable to achieve a goal we were not destined to reach! How do we test our calling and purpose?

1. *The affirmation of others:* We need to find mature Christians who are willing to provide counsel and/or accountability as we seek our personal destiny. If at any time thy don't affirm what we believe to be God's call, we need to be cautious and, together with them, prayerfully reexamine our direction.

2. *Compatibility with gifting:* The Holy Spirit, according to First Corinthians, has given gifts to us at His discretion. Whatever God calls us to do, we can be sure it will coincide with our spiritual gifts. If a man who is five feet tall and weighs one hundred forty-five pounds announces he wants to be the next champion Sumo wrestler, those who really love him might want to try and talk him out of it. Many Christians haven't any idea

where their spiritual giftings lie. That makes for a difficult time trying to determine destiny.

3. *Know your purpose:* For too long we have separated our lives into sacred and secular categories. Both the man praying in the temple to the man plowing in the field are to be "Holy unto the Lord." Because a person is a missionary on a mission field, it does not give the greater opportunity to glorify God any more than an entrepreneur building their own business. As long as they both use their gifts and opportunities to glorify God by serving people. If your sense of destiny is in the market place, then stop looking in other directions for your fulfillment. Christ desires pre-eminence in your life, period. Even if you're a scuba diver for Roto Rooter, you can reach people in your realm of influence. Settle it and quit casting your eyes on another man's field. Bloom where you're planted!!!

DIFFICULT CIRCUMSTANCES

Paul Harvey said, "You can tell you're on the road to success. It's uphill all the way." Jesus told His disciples, *"In this world you will have tribulation, but be of good cheer, for I have overcome the world."* (John 16:33) Difficult circumstances only become demonic delays when we allow them to cause us to slow the pace or even quit. Doc Holliday's character in the movie *Tombstone* said, "There are no normal lives, there's just life. Go live it, and don't let it get to you." We sometimes live with the impression that the life of the servant of God is supposed to go a certain way. Difficult circumstances must be seen as challenges to allow the glory of God to be seen!

"But we have this treasure in earthen vessels,
that the excellence of the power may be of

God and not of us . We are hard-pressed on
every side, yet not crushed; we are perplexed,
but not in despair; persecuted, but not
forsaken; struck down, but not destroyed
-- always carrying about in the body the
dying of the Lord Jesus, that the life of Jesus
may be made manifest in our body. For we
which live are always delivered unto death for
Jesus' sake, that the life of Jesus also may be
manifested in our mortal flesh. So then death
is working in us, but life in you. And since
we have the same spirit of faith, according
to what is written,'I believed, and therefor I
spoke,' we also believe, and therefore speak,
knowing that he who raised up the Lord
Jesus will also raise us up with Jesus, and will
present us with you. For all things are for
your sakes, that grace, having spread through
the many, may cause thanksgiving to abound
to the glory of God." (II Corinthians 4:7-15)

UNRESOLVED CONFLICT

Again, this demonic delay may find it's source in either those around us or in our own minds. Conflict with those around us which goes unresolved is like a parasitic condition in which the very life's blood of vision is siphoned from us. We cannot function in the grace of God if the grace of God does not function in us. Relationships are vital to the fulfillment of vision. No vision which is truly of God is small enough to be accomplished by one person acting alone. Conflict is inevitable, but if it is unresolved it will delay or destroy our destiny.

Conflict within ourselves, however, is even more insidious. In fact, it is the source of all conflict with others. The more at peace we are with ourselves, the more at peace we are with those around us. If the peace of God "rules" our hearts (Colossians 3:15), it will govern our relationships. The meaning of the word "rule" in this passage could be compared to our word "umpire." The peace of God will tell us whether or not we are "in the strike zone," or if we are "fair" or "foul." We treat others generally how we feel about ourselves.

Our Mental Attitude

Our mental approach to the detours of life can determine the length and severity of the delay. There are at least three mental attitudes which can quickly erode our ability to release our full potential.

■ **Procrastination. James 4:14 says,** *"Whereas you do not know what will happen tomorrow. For what is your life? It is even as a vapor that appears for a little time and then vanishes away." "The great day of the LORD is near, it is near and hastens quickly."* **(Zephaniah 1:14a) Procrastination is not just a character issue. Where destiny and the will of God is concerned, it's a spiritual warfare issue. The spirit of slothfulness attempts to lull us into thinking we have all the time in the world to accomplish what God has spoken. Don't put off dealing with procrastination!**

> ### Aspire to inspire before you expire

■ **Discouragement.** *"Therefore, my beloved brethren, be ye steadfast, immoveable, always abounding in the work of the Lord, knowing that your labor is not in vain in the Lord."* **(1 Corinthians 15:58) Again, this is an attack designed to keep us from living in God's calling. David spoke to himself (yes, it's alright to talk to yourself if you speak positive things), and said,** *"Why are you* *cast down, O my soul? And why are you disquieted within me? Hope in God: for I shall yet praise Him for the help of His countenance."* **(Psalms 42:5)**

■ **Doubt.** *"But without faith it is impossible to please Him: for he that cometh to God must believe that he is, and that he is a rewarder of them that diligently seek him."* **(Hebrews 11:6) Also, in Matthew 21:21-22 we read,** *"Jesus answered and said unto them, Verily I say unto you, If ye have faith, and doubt not, ye shall not only do this which is done to the fig tree, but also if ye shall say unto this mountain, Be thou removed, and be thou cast into the sea; it shall be done. And all things, whatsoever ye shall ask in prayer, believing, ye shall receive."* **Doubt is a destroyer of vision. Henry Ford is credited with saying, "Whether you think you can or you think you can't, you're probably right."**

OUR ADVERSARY

As we have said, many of the things we think of as inner soul issues actually have a very real root in the work of the Enemy in our lives. Our failure to allow God to control any aspect of us becomes an open door for strongholds to be built. Remember, some detours may be divine (more on that later), but many delays are demonic. When Joshua was leading the Children of Israel, the enemy threw up a roadblock at Ai.

> *"But the children of Israel committed a trespass in the accursed thing: for Achan, the son of Carmi, the son of Zabdi, the son of Zerah, of the tribe of Judah, took of the accursed thing: and the anger of the LORD was kindled against the children of Israel.*

And Joshua sent men from Jericho to Ai,
which is beside Bethaven, on the east side of
Bethel, and spake unto them, saying, Go up
and view the country. And the men went up
and viewed Ai. And they returned to Joshua,
and said unto him, Let not all the people go
up; but let about two or three thousand men
go up and smite Ai; and make not all the
people to labour thither; for they are but few.
So there went up thither of the people about
three thousand men: and they fled before the
men of Ai." (Joshua 7:1-5)

If the devil's forces aren't strong enough for a frontal attack, he'll try subterfuge. Most of our problems with either overt or subtle attacks by the Enemy are due to underestimating his cunning and tenacity. He will try everything and stop at nothing. This is exactly the reason scripture has strong words of warning:

"Be sober, be vigilant; because your adversary
the devil, as a roaring lion, walketh about,
seeking whom he may devour: Whom resist
steadfast in the faith, knowing that the same
afflictions are accomplished in your brethren
that are in the world." (1 Peter 5:8-9)

I do, however, want to add that while he does go about as a roaring lion, you have the strong lion of the tribe of Judah (Jesus) living in you. And greater is he that is in you than he who is in the world.

DIVINE DETOURS

Graham Cooke, author of *Developing Your Prophetic Gifting*, has well said, "God is much more interested in what we become than what we accomplish." Since that is true, it is a small thing to God if He knows that the development of our character requires a side trip or two along the way to destiny. It's the *process* of becoming mature saints that God is after, more than the final outcome. We may fret and fuss about these detours, but God smiles and enjoys them, for He knows what, through them, we are becoming!

As was covered in detail in chapter two, Joseph experienced divine detours along the path to his destiny as a ruler and leader. His God-given dream from childhood was several years and many "pitfalls" from completion. At the end of the day, however, Joseph was clear about the process:

> *"But as for you, ye thought evil against me;*
> *but God meant it unto good, to bring to pass,*
> *as it is this day, to save much people alive."*
> (Genesis 50:20)

From his dream revealed, to the pit, into slavery, on to Potiphar's house, into prison, and finally the second highest throne in the land, Joseph had seen the hand of the Lord at every turn. We never read of him railing against God, feeling forsaken or giving up. Though there must have been times when he wondered what God was up to, he kept the vision before him until his vision became reality. To ask God a question, you may, but to question God, you must not.

When we face a point in our journey where it doesn't seem we can go forward any further, how can we know if we are encountering a divine detour or a demonic delay?

First, remember the promise of our Lord of His everlasting

presence. He will never leave us or forsake us. He is with us to the end of the age. Four times in the story of Joseph we read, "And the Lord was with Joseph." Present circumstances may seem to indicate we are the victim of evil, and in fact, that may have been the intent. Our assurance that God sees this as a divine detour is that His presence and blessing is evident in spite of our situation. Because, we know that all things work together for our good and his glory.

Second, when we examine our motives and our actions leading to our present predicament, we can be confident of God's guiding hand, if we know we have conducted ourselves with character and integrity. In other words, we've done the right thing. Joseph ended up in jail for doing the right thing. The only thing that will get us through times of accusation, allegation and criticism is the sure knowledge that we can look into the mirror and into the face of God with confident assurance that we did what was right.

WHAT SHOULD OUR ATTITUDE BE WHILE ON A DIVINE DETOUR?

Faithfulness. Joseph remained true to his Lord and to his vision and never quit.

Blessing. Even concerning those who mistreated him, Joseph chose to use his gifting for their good.

Forgiveness. While we struggle with this area, we see that it simply wasn't an issue with Joseph. He never considered unforgiveness as an option, as far as we know. He certainly never thought about revenge.

Restoration. The reunion of Joseph with his brothers, and later with his father, was almost more than he could have hoped for. Joseph was so glad to see his family, he had to turn away from them so they wouldn't discover his identity!

Detours have caused many to leave the road to destiny far short of the goal. Discouragement, confusion and despair will bring about the loss of our dream. We must guard our dreams and visions at all cost. Remember, God's ways are not our ways. Rather than railing at the detour signs, let's explore the side route expecting God to show us wondrous truths along the way.

CHAPTER 9

Coping With Criticism
Respond Don't React

One of the first lessons you learned as a leader is that criticism is a fact of life. You can run from it, hide under your bed, and hope it will go away, but it never does. The best way to deal with it, like dealing with problems, is to learn the "right" way to handle it.

> Webster says: "criticize"...1. To consider the merits and demerits of and judge accordingly; evaluate. 2. To stress the faults of; Syn: Reprehend; Blame; Censure; Condemn; Denounce; Criticize implies finding fault especially with methods or policies or intentions.

We are a nation of critics: We have art critics, food critics, movie critics, political critics, and even church critics. Everyone gets in on the action. All you have to do is tune in to your favorite radio talk show and you can hear that we have become a nation of experts on every topic you can imagine. It really doesn't matter if you've never played the game, or run for public office, or been the CEO of a large corporation, just give your opinion, offer your criticism, and now you're an expert on the subject.

> **"He has the right to criticize who has the heart to help."**
> **— Abraham Lincoln**

There is no doubt that some people offer criticism, because they genuinely want to help. The problem is twofold:
- **They don't know how to give it**
- **We don't know how to receive it**

That doesn't make them a bad person, and it doesn't make us immune to receive it. Just like anything else we deal with in life, there is a "right" way to give it and a better, more constructive way to receive it.

> *A successful person is one who can lay a firm*
> *foundation with the bricks that others throw*
> *at him or her.* (David Brinkley)

Since criticism is a fact of life, and there is no way to stop it, it's best that we learn how to "cope" with it, grow from the knowledge, and let it be our teacher instead of our master.

WHY DO SUCCESSFUL LEADERS FACE CRITICISM

1. BECAUSE PEOPLE FEEL THEY HAVE A RIGHT!

Some people would rather stand in the background and wait for you to become successful, and then criticize you. They wait until you look like you have finally "made it" and then throw water in your face to cool you down. They don't care how hard you worked, or how much investment you've made. Their goal is to bring you down when it looks like you're getting to far ahead.

"The Higher you Rise, the More you are Criticized"

LOOK AT WHAT HAPPENED TO JOSEPH.
- **He was hated by his brothers for being a dreamer. (Gen.37:4-5)**
- **He had "negative words" spoken against him. (Gen.37:23-36)**

■ He ends up in a Pit and sold into slavery (Gen.37:23-24)

2. BECAUSE PEOPLE GET JEALOUS!

It's called the "lead dog" principle. You know the old saying, "If you're not the lead dog the view never changes." They can do a better job, so they are always heaping criticism on you. It's always something: You're too young, too old, or you don't have enough education, you haven't been in business long enough or you haven't paid "your dues." You name it and the critics will come up with something to say.

3. BECAUSE IT COMES WITH SUCCESS!

The best way to avoid criticism is - do nothing, say nothing, and be nothing! Then someone will come along and criticize you for wasting your talent! The greatest men and women of the Bible and human history were criticized, so you're in good company.

THINK ABOUT THIS:
"The horse is here to stay, but the automobile is only a novelty, a fad."

—The President of the Michigan Savings Bank advising Henry Ford's lawyer not to invest in the Ford Motor Co., 1903. Henry Ford was 40 years old when he founded the Ford Motor Company, which would go on to become one of the world's largest and most profitable companies.

"How, sir, would you make a ship sail against the wind and currents by lighting a bonfire under her deck? I pray you, excuse me, I have not the time to listen to such nonsense."

—Napoleon Bonaparte, when told of Robert Fulton's steamboat plans, 1800s.

"Everyone acquainted with the subject will recognize it as a conspicuous failure."

—Henry Morton, President of the Stevens Institute of Technology, on Edison's light bulb, 1880.

"There is no reason anyone would want a computer in their home."
—Ken Olson, Founder of Digital Equipment Corp., 1977.

At a recent pastor's retreat, each minister in attendance was asked the following question: "How many people does it take to screw in a light bulb?" The answers were as follows. A Presbyterian Pastor responded, "None. If God wants the bulb screwed in, he is sovereign and will do it himself without human effort." A Charismatic Pastor replied, "None. The bulb doesn't need to be changed. We should pray that it be healed." A Pentecostal Pastor said, "None. We simply need to cast out from the bulb the demon of darkness." The Fundamentalist Pastor stated, "None. We shouldn't even enter the room because we need to keep ourselves separate from all darkness." A Baptist Pastor responded, "None. If we allow physical contact between a person and the bulb it might lead to dancing." The Wesleyan Minister replied, "None. If we just show the bulb its need, it already possesses the power to screw itself in." A Non-Denominational

Pastor said, "None. We don't want to make the bulb feel unwanted or uncomfortable." This poll provides one clear conclusion: It's no wonder pastors are always in the dark.

4. **BECAUSE CHANGE REPRESENTS A THREAT!**

As a leader, you represent change. Whether you view yourself as a change agent or not, as a leader, that's what you represent. For the most part, people fear change, so who will they attack? YOU!

Simply because of who you are, the very nature of your position opens you up to criticism. Whether we like it or not, it comes with the territory.

Read the book of Nehemiah and consider the things he had to endure in order to complete his mission:

- **He was called a rebel**
- **He refused to talk to his enemies**
- **He was accused of wanting to be King**
- **It was said that he was not being very Spiritual**
- **His enemies even tried to kill him**

It seemed that every time he turned around, he was faced with criticism and complaining. Not only from his enemies, but also from those who were suppose to be his leaders.

Nehemiah was a change agent. I'm sure he didn't view himself that way. If you had asked him he would have told you all he was trying to do was rebuild the walls around Jerusalem, nothing more, nothing less.

Ask yourself these important questions:

1. **IS ALL CRITICISM WRONG OR BAD?**
2. **DON'T WE BRING SOME OF IT ON OURSELVES BY DOING "DUMB THINGS?"**
3. **CAN'T WE LEARN FROM OUR CRITICS?**

"Faithful are the wounds of a friend; but the kisses of an enemy are deceitful." (Pro.27:6)

Ten Ways To Handle Criticism

1. **LEARN THE DIFFERENCE BETWEEN "CONSTRUCTIVE" AND "DESTRUCTIVE" CRITICISM**

Constructive Criticism is when I criticize you.

Destructive Criticism is when you criticize me.

Let's be honest, most of us don't mind giving criticism to just about anyone who will listen. It's easy to give it and very hard to receive it.

How do you know when it's constructive or destructive? Ask three questions:

■ **How was it given?**

Everybody wants the benefit of the doubt, right? It's hard to take criticism when we feel the person giving it does not have our best interest at heart.

As a minister, for more years than I care to count, I know what it's like to be confronted and criticized with a judgmental spirit. Believe me it's, no fun. When faced with it, I didn't know if the person was just trying to hurt me or help me.

■ **Where was it given?**

You know the sick feeling you get in your stomach when you witness a parent screaming at their child in the mall or any public place? How many times have we said, "I'd never do that?" We might not do that to our children, but adults do it to each other all the time. Whether in the workplace, at school or on the practice field, it happens all the time.

Personally, I have found that private talk is much better than public confrontation. Usually our first reaction to criticism is to defend ourselves, and being confronted in public only makes matters worse.

■ **From their personal frustration and fear — or for your growth?**

Friends want to see us grow even when they say a "hard" thing to us. The key word is "friend." I don't believe you have the right to criticize someone who is not a true friend. That may sound strange, but if you don't have a relationship with that person, they are not going to hear you at all. And if you don't care if they hear you, or your words of criticism are not going to make them a better person, then all you're doing is venting your personal frustration onto them.

One thing the critic wants to do is get an emotional response from you. Of course, that would be anger. People who criticize normally want an argument to happen. After they say something rude or mean, they expect you to retaliate by defending yourself. If you do this, an argument will most likely occur. Do not try to argue with a person like this. There is no way for you to defend yourself, so let him believe what he wants to, because chances are, he will anyway.

2. DON'T TAKE YOURSELF TOO SERIOUSLY

It's hard to imagine, but the whole world does not depend on you. That's right, somehow, someway, the world will go on with or without you. However, the truth is, we want you around to contribute your gifts and talents to all of us.

Research has shown that the health benefits of laughter are far-ranging. While more studies need to be done, studies so far have shown that laughter can help relieve pain, bring greater happiness and even increase immunity.

Did You Know that Laughter Can Reduce Stress?

Hormones: Laughter reduces the level of stress hormones like cortisol, epinephrine (adrenaline), dopamine and growth hormone. It also increases the level of health-enhancing hormones like endorphins and neurotransmitters. Laughter increases the number of antibody-producing cells and enhances the effectiveness of T cells. All this means a stronger immune system as well as fewer physical effects of stress.

Physical Release: Have you ever felt like you "have to laugh or you'll cry?" Have you experienced the cleansed feeling after a good laugh? Laughter provides a physical and emotional release.

Internal Workout: A good belly laugh exercises the diaphragm, contracts the abs and even works out the shoulders, leaving muscles more relaxed afterward. It even provides a good workout for the heart.

Distraction: Laughter brings the focus away from anger, guilt, stress and negative emotions in a more beneficial way than other mere distractions.

Perspective: Studies show that our response to stressful events can be altered by whether we view something as a 'threat' or a 'challenge'. Humor can give us a more lighthearted perspective and help us view events as 'challenges', thereby making them less threatening and more positive. (For more on changing your perspective, see this article on cognitive reframing).

Social Benefits of Laughter: Laughter connects us with others. Just as with smiling and kindness, most people find that laughter is contagious, so if you bring more laughter into your life, you can most likely help others around you to laugh more, and realize these benefits as well. By elevating the mood of those around you, you can reduce their stress levels and perhaps improve the quality of social interaction you experience with them reducing your stress level even more!

> *Try to make at least one person happy every day, and then in ten years you may have made three thousand, six hundred and fifty persons happy or brightened a small town by your contribution to the fund of general enjoyment.* (Sydney Smith)

3. **CONSIDER THE SOURCE**

Jennifer VanBaren, eHow Contributor says,

> "Understand this type of person and why he acts this way. Normally, a happy person does not criticize others in a hurtful way. People who constantly criticize often do this to cover up their own insecurities and make them feel better about themselves. They are often people who have suffered a lot of pain in their lives and use this as a type of defense toward others. When you are criticized by someone, before you get angry at them, take the time to reflect on what was said. Maybe there is something that you can learn from that criticism."

Ask yourself this question: Is the person who is giving me the criticism trying to help me reach my potential? If so, calm down and listen. If not, thank them for their advice, learn what you can from it and move on.

It's important to remember, not everyone who is offering criticism is trying to destroy you.

One of the first lessons I learned is that criticism is a fact of life. I didn't like it one bit! I thought everyone would love me, especially for my wonderful personality and speaking ability. Little did I realize, I was not the favorite that I thought I was?

There was a Pastor I knew who was so arrogant that he announced to the congregation that he was going to take a year and preach through the whole Bible. He just couldn't understand why everyone didn't applaud. Finally, an old deacon took him aside and said, "Son, I've been alive for over eighty years and studied the Bible over fifty, and I haven't even scratched the surface." The young Pastor just smiled and thanked him. After a year, and not even through the book of Genesis, he went back to the old deacon and told him how foolish he must have sounded. The deacon just smiled and said, "Don't worry about it son, you have many more years to make many more mistakes." OUCH!

> It is better to hear the rebuke of the wise
> than for a man to hear the song of fools.
> (Ecclesiastes 7:5)

4. YOUR ATTITUDE IS EVERYTHING

Sometimes, we want to kill the critic. That would be a "bad" attitude, wouldn't you say? Correction can come in many shapes and sizes. Sometimes, it may even come from someone you don't like or respect.

Our first reaction is usually wrong. We defend ourselves.

Sometimes, we even lash back. It's a natural thing to do. Once we get over our wounded pride, maybe we can sit down and take inventory to see if there is any truth to what we heard.

> *"Better a patient man than a warrior, a man who controls his temper than one who takes a city."* (Proverbs 16:32)

We can handle criticism with a positive attitude

- Take a deep breath and give it a little thought
- Turn a negative into a positive
- Make something useful out of the criticism
- Heap coals of fire on their head — bless them, don't curse them
- Learn from the criticism
- Take the high road — be the better person

There's a direct correlation between a positive attitude, better relationships, superior health and greater success. A positive attitude can boost your energy, heighten your inner strength, inspire others, and garner the fortitude to meet difficult challenges. According to research from the Mayo Clinic, positive thinking can increase your life span, decrease depression, reduce levels of distress, provide greater resistance to the common cold, offer better psychological and physical well-being, reduce the risk of death from cardiovascular disease, and enable you to cope better during hardships and times of stress. (Frank K. Sonnenberg)

5. **REMEMBER THE LORD JESUS**
Consider what they did to the greatest leader who ever lived.

■ **Called a <u>glutton</u>**

> *The Son of Man came eating and drinking, and they say, 'Here is a glutton and a drunkard, a friend of tax collectors and sinners. But wisdom is proved right by her actions."* (Matt 11:19)

■ **Called a <u>drunk</u> (Matt.11:19))**

■ **Accused of hanging out with the wrong <u>crowd</u>**

> *And when the Pharisees saw it, they said to His disciples, "Why does your Teacher eat with tax collectors and sinners?"* (Matt 9:11)

■ **They said He had a <u>demon</u>.**
> *Then the Jews answered and said to Him, "Do we not say rightly that You are a Samaritan and have a demon?"* (John 8:48, NKJ)

■ **They said He was <u>crazy</u>.**

But when His own people heard about this,
they went out to lay hold of Him, for they
said, "He is out of His mind." (Mark 3:21)

> **If they did that to Him,**
> **what do you think they will do to you?**

6. STAY IN PHYSICAL AND SPIRITUAL SHAPE

Criticism, when we are running on empty, causes us to see it with a distorted view. You can't keep going without it affecting you.

In his excellent book "Running on Empty" author Fil Anderson states:

"Sometimes the only way to get a new life is by running your old one completely into the ground. My frenetic pace of ministry gave me just one thing: greater pressure to do even more. I fell for the soul killing lie that doing more is what matters, and what I needed was to stop living 'for' God and start living 'with' Him."

THINK ABOUT ELIJAH

He had it all going for him. He was a strong prophet, standing tall on top of the mountain. You could say he wasn't afraid of anybody. Something strange happens to him on his way to greatness. He ran away from a woman and even wanted to commit suicide. Why? There has been much speculation as to the reason he ended up running away to the desert. But, for me, one of the main reasons Elijah had a breakdown was mental and physical fatigue. He won a great victory over the forces of Baal, and yet when he got a note from Jezebel, he was filled with fear and took off running. With the help of a few angels, he got himself straightened out, but it took some time. He needed rest, refreshment and a strong, encouraging word from the Lord.

When we are running nonstop, not taking care of ourselves physically, we are more prone to let criticism affect us in a negative way. Have you noticed when you are in good shape you can handle things better than when you feel "run down" and ready to crash and burn? Don't fall into the black hole of despair like Elijah did. Get moving and watch things improve.

> Physical fitness is not only one of the most
> important keys to a healthy body; it is the
> basis of dynamic and creative intellectual
> activity. (John F. Kennedy)

7. LOOK BEYOND THE CRITIC

One way to handle criticism is to ask yourself, "Do I hear this from others or just one person?" Many times, when a person comes to you with criticism and says "they said," it usually means, "I'm really saying this, but I'm afraid to tell you." A lot of times the person talking to you doesn't have the courage to tell you what they really think. They will use the excuse that it's not "them" but "they" who said it. At the end of the day, it doesn't matter whether it was "them" or "they." Stay focused on the goal of becoming the person God intended you to be.

> "Belief in oneself is one of the most
> important bricks in building any successful
> venture." (Lydia M. Child)

> Develop success from failures.
> Discouragement and failure are two of the
> surest stepping stones to success.
> (Dale Carnegie)

How often do you find people who accept the bricks thrown at them and still are able to build a strong foundation? Just one or two in hundreds, we assume. All of us are criticized at one time or another. In fact, if you are one of those highly creative and distinguished people who are committed to excellence, you are bound to be surrounded by countless critics. This criticism generally occurs when you consider making excellence your goal, accepting a leadership position, taking a stand, sharing your faith, not compromising on your principles, speaking out or implementing a change. Face it, when you step out, reaching for your goals, there will be someone standing on the sidelines waiting to "cool" you off.

8. TIME IS ON YOUR SIDE

As you get older you learn some things. One lesson learned is that you don't have to have an answer for every time you are criticized, even though the tendency is to defend and then attack. The better approach is to get quiet, and if you are right and the critic wrong, time will prove it for you.

Jesus had a way to get "under the skin" of his critics. Many times when they attacked He would just stay silent for a while. When He did answer, it was not what they were looking for.

Go ahead. Throw something!

But Jesus went to the Mount of Olives. 2
Early in the morning He came again into the
temple, and all the people were coming to
Him; and He sat down and began to teach
them. 3 The scribes and the Pharisees brought
a woman caught in adultery, and having set
her in the center of the court, 4 they said to

Him, "Teacher, this woman has been caught in adultery, in the very act. 5 Now in the Law, Moses commanded us to stone such women; what then do you say?" 6 They were saying this, testing Him, so that they might have grounds for accusing Him. But Jesus stooped down and with His finger wrote on the ground. 7 but when they persisted in asking Him, He straightened up, and said to them, "He who is without sin among you, let him be the first to throw a stone at her." 8 Again He stooped down and wrote on the ground. 9 When they heard it, they began to go out one by one, beginning with the older ones, and He was left alone, and the woman, where she was, in the center of the court. 10 Straightening up, Jesus said to her, "Woman, where are they? Did no one condemn you?" 11 She said, "No one, Lord." And Jesus said, "I do not condemn you, either. Go. From now on sin no more." (John 8:1-11)

Jesus knew how to deal with criticism. Instead of attacking the crowd, He waited and then asked this question, "He who is without sin among you, let him be the first to throw a stone at her." That got their attention. He was saying, "You who are so quick to criticize and judge, be the first to throw something at her." He stopped them cold, and they turned and walked away.

The next time you are faced with sharp and biting criticism try the "Jesus approach."

9. HANG AROUND WITH POSITIVE PEOPLE

If you hang around "garbage collectors" guess what you will become? That's right: A land fill. What would you do if your neighbor decided to dump his garbage on your lawn? I'm sure you would find that unpleasant and uncalled for. No doubt you would call the authorities and have action taken. Every time we allow someone to "dump" their negativity into our soul it will eventually affect how we think, feel and act. If you constantly allow your circle of friends to complain and tear down everyone and everything, guess what you will become? Just like them!

Positive people are one of life's greatest joys. If you are looking forward to creating a better life for yourself, this is another way to make that better life a reality. There are two major reasons why you should make the effort to be around positive people as much as possible:

> **Being around positive people makes you feel good and builds self confidence**

The most obvious reason to be around positive people is that being around positive people makes you feel good. Positive people are the people who offer you emotional support when you are having issues in your life. Positive people are the kinds of people that you can have a good laugh with. You can smile with them, and you can also encourage them to become better people and set a good example for others. Positive people have great reasons for wanting to live. Positive people view life as a gift and try to make the most of what they have. Positive people practice gratitude on a regular basis. Instead of complaining, positive people try to find reasons to smile, even if they are having problems in their life. But the first step must be taken by you. You have got to make the effort to hang around positive people as much as you can. They will greatly improve and enrich your life. That is how great the impact of being around positive people is. You cannot put a price on feeling good, because feeling good is priceless.

> ## Being around positive people
> ## improves the quality of your life

Research and numerous studies have shown that people who are positive and associate themselves with positive people benefit from these interactions in many ways. By being around positive people you will be healthier, more successful financially and you will be involved in better relationships. Being around positive people lowers your stress level, and it enables you to relax more. If you are low on stress that means that your body does not have to work as hard and you will be healthier as result. Positive people are more likely to get job promotions. This results in the person getting paid more money and becoming more successful financially. If you hang around positive people, you will attract by default more positive people to you. That is the way it is designed, because what you regularly focus on you will attract. Being around positive people means that other people will see how positive you are, and they will want to be around you. As a result, the quality of your relationships will be enriched and made so much better by you making that simple choice to be around positive people.

"He who walks with wise men will be wise."
(Proverbs 13:19)

10. FOCUS ON YOUR PURPOSE
Remember, you have an enemy. It's not people (flesh and blood). The Enemy knows just how to "get to you" and knock you off track. It's so easy to lose focus and forget what we are supposed to be doing.

We can get so caught up with criticism that we stop short of our intended target.

> "It is a mistake to look too far ahead. Only
> one link of the chain of destiny can be
> handled at a time." (Winston Churchill)

Don't let constant criticism take you away from your path. If you are not careful, you will spend more time on what the critics say than what God says about your future. If you do, you can end up going in the wrong direction.

On 17 July 1938, Douglas Corrigan took off from Brooklyn's Floyd Bennett airfield in a tiny single-engine plane. Corrigan had filed a flight plan for California, but 29 hours later he arrived in Ireland, claiming his compasses had failed, and that he had accidentally flown the wrong way. Although Corrigan never quite admitted it, his 'mistake' was surely a ruse to circumvent aviation authorities who had turned down his request to make a trans-Atlantic flight. Corrigan's stunt caught the public fancy; he was given a hero's welcome on his return to New York and "Wrong-Way Corrigan" became a popular nickname for anyone who made a big blunder or did things backwards. Corrigan published his biography, That's My Story, in 1938.

CHAPTER 10

The Past is Past
It's Time To Run!

In life, we know that timing is everything. Whether it's hitting a baseball, catching a flight, standing on the first tee or closing a business deal. It's all about timing. How many people have said, "I wish I had more time?"

Time can be a wonderful friend or an avowed enemy. Time will even talk to you and say things like – "You're running out of time" or "You don't have enough time," or worse yet, "Don't do it now, you've got plenty of time." It will convince you that you will never have enough time to plan properly, execute wisely and follow through completely. If you don't understand how important time is and the strategic moments of your life, you will end up wondering, like so many others, "where did all my time go?"

> **Time is the scarcest resource; and unless it is managed, nothing else can be managed." (Peter F. Drucker)**

The greatest collection of creative ideas, inventions and business never started, are not found in the market place, or in a church – but in the local cemetery. Why? Because many people never follow through with their ideas or creative instincts. They just die still thinking they have plenty of time.

DIE EMPTY

The great Apostle Paul said it best when he said, "I have fought the good fight, I have finished the race, I have kept the faith."

Paul was a man who "finished" everything he set out to do, with nothing left to prove, and nothing left to do. As they say in the sports world, "He left everything on the field." Paul died empty! When our time is up, may it be said of us that we, too, left everything on the field of life with nothing left to prove and no regrets with how we used the most precious commodity we have, and that is our time. Life is a journey and not a destination. But, we need to have a sense every day that, should we die that day, we have lived to our capacities.

In the workplace, the only real thing you have to exchange is your experience and your time. In our society, we function based on money. When you get your paycheck you have just exchanged your "time" for the companies' money. I'm sure you would agree then, that time is a pretty important factor in every facet of our lives. Your time, plus your effort, creates your volume of productivity that produces lifestyle (money, bonuses and trips).

525,600

That's how many minutes are in a year — What are you planning on doing with them? A year from now, you will be the same person you are right now, if you don't make a decision to do something with those 525,600 minutes. This may be shocking to you, but we all have the same amount. That's right! Whether you're Bill Gates or the guy that makes your coffee at Startbucks, it's the same amount. God is not making any more of it, so we need to learn use it wisely.

THE BIBLE HAS A LOT TO SAY ABOUT TIME.

First, there is CHRONOS (Times) and second, there is KAIROS (seasons).

These two words are the ones most commonly used to describe what we call "time."

Chronos—or Standard Time

This is where we get our English word Chronology. This is the general process of time. This is the day to day events. This is time we spend getting up, going to work, taking the kids to school, preparing supper – you know all those things that we think are not very important. In fact, what we might call unimportant, God thinks is very important. I'm convinced that everything we do has a purpose. It's all a part of our preparation. It's in the day to day routine of life that we are being prepared for something greater. There is an age old principle that says, "If God can't trust me in the little things, how can He trust me with greater things."

> **When the door of opportunity opens, it's too late to prepare!**

> "A pessimist is one who makes difficulties
> of his opportunities, and an optimist is one
> who makes opportunities of his difficulties."
> (Harry S. Truman)

Kairos—Strategic Time

This refers to the "right" time, the opportune or strategic time, the "now" moments of our life.

One thing I've learned about the Lord is, He seems to be more interested in "timing" than "time." We ask Him for things. We pray, and we cry, and if He doesn't answer in the next ten minutes, we give up, get mad and never ask anything again. How many times have we asked for something that we were not ready to handle and never considered the fact that God knew best? So, if your latest creative idea has not taken off, you've soaked it in prayer, received wise counsel, did all the backbreaking ground work, and still nothing has happened, cheer up, it's all a matter of God's timing for you.

Take a trip down memory lane with me.

There was a couple in the Bible named Zacharias and Elizabeth. For years, they had prayed for a son and nothing ever happened. There is no doubt in my mind they had given up and decided God was never going to answer their heart's desire for a baby.

Like many of us, they looked at the calendar, and with each birthday knew that "time" was against them. As you read the story you realize that with God, it's a "timing" issue.

One day while serving in the temple, an Angel appeared to Zacharias and announced that Elizabeth was going to give birth to a son, even telling him his name. Can you imagine the shock!? Why? They were old, and besides that, they had already given up. Yet, the miracle they were longing for so many years before was now coming to pass.

How could this be? The key statement in the whole story is found in the statement of the Angel when he said, "Do not be afraid, Zacharias, for your prayer is (was) heard, and your wife Elizabeth will bear you a son, and you shall call his name John." Literally, the Angel was saying, "from the first day you and your wife prayed for a son God decided to answer you. But God didn't need you to have a son, then, He needs you to have your son, now. It's all tied to God's divine "timing."

WHAT LESSONS CAN WE GLEAN FROM THIS GREAT BIBLE STORY?

■ Sometimes God delays the answer to give something better

- Sometimes God delays until the situation is impossible, so then our faith is in Him alone.
- Sometimes God delays the answer until it is linked to Divine necessity

> **God will always give us His best when we leave the choice up to Him!**

"Dost thou love life? Then do not squander time, for that's the stuff life is made of." (Benjamin Franklin, *Poor Richard's Almanac*)

As Christians, we go through many "times" and "seasons"

Think about a few of them:

1. **Seasons of Rest and Refreshment -**

   The LORD is my shepherd, I shall not be in want. He makes me lie down in green pastures, he leads me beside quiet waters, he restores my soul. He guides me in paths of righteousness for his name's sake. (Psalms 23:1-3)

2. **Seasons when we are in the Desert and Dry.**

   See, I am doing a new thing! Now it springs up; do you not perceive it? I am making a way in the desert and streams in the wasteland. The wild animals honor me, the jackals and the owls, because I provide water in the desert and streams in the wasteland, to give drink to my people, my chosen, (Isaiah 43:19-20)

For I will pour water on the thirsty land, and streams on the dry ground; I will pour out my Spirit on your offspring, and my blessing on your descendants. (Isaiah 44:3)

3. **SEASONS WHEN IT'S TIME TO WAIT AND BE QUIET.**
   He gives strength to the weary and increases the power of the weak.Even youths grow tired and weary, and young men stumble and fall; but those who hope in the LORD will renew their strength. They will soar on wings like eagles; they will run and not grow weary, they will walk and not be faint.
   (Isaiah 40:29-31)

One of the ways to describe the believer is like a "runner." Once we finally understand that life is not a "play ground" but a" battle ground," we can then move forward and not look back at past failures and disappointments.

Does anybody know what time it is? — It's time to run!!!

RUN —
- **Toward Your Commitments**
- **Your Purpose and Destiny**
- **To Promises you have made to yourself and to others**
  Do you not know that in a race all the runners run, but only one gets the prize? Run

in such a way as to get the prize. Everyone who competes in the games goes into strict training. They do it to get a crown that will not last; but we do it to get a crown that will last forever. Therefore I do not run like a man running aimlessly; I do not fight like a man beating the air. No, I beat my body and make it my slave so that after I have preached to others, I myself will not be disqualified for the prize. (1 Cor 9:24-27)

But the main focus is on this Scripture in Hebrews 12:

Therefore, since we are surrounded by such a great cloud of witnesses, let us throw off everything that hinders and the sin that so easily entangles, and let us run with perseverance the race marked out for us. Let us fix our eyes on Jesus, the author and perfecter of our faith, who for the joy set before him endured the cross, scorning its shame, and sat down at the right hand of the throne of God. Consider him who endured such opposition from sinful men, so that you will not grow weary and lose heart. (Heb 12:1-3)

The Arena in Which We Run

Therefore, since we are surrounded by such a great cloud of witnesses, let us throw off

everything that hinders (weight) and the sin
that so easily entangles, and let us run with
perseverance the race marked out for us.
(Heb 12:1)

The Context

The writer of Hebrews had just finished talking about the heroes of faith in chapter11. He is letting us know that we are not alone. Others have gone on before and run the race set before them. He knew we would need encouragement and endurance for the race. Everyone needs encouragement. There are times in our lives when nothing seems to go well. For many, that is the time they give up on their dreams and vow to never again attempt anything new or different. To be discouraged is a hard thing to deal with, but it can be done. How?

- **Remember the good things in your past**
- **Always know that this too shall come to pass, it's only temporary**
- **Always know that Discouragement is an emotion, not a fact of life**

> **Correction does much, but encouragement does more.**
> **(Johann Wolfgang von Goethe)**

The Crowd

On one side we have Jesus at the finish line cheering us on: The author and finisher of our faith. He knew what it was like to be cheered one minute and hated the next. He kept on running toward the prize in spite of all that was against Him. I'm so glad that Jesus did not act like so many today, at the first sign of trouble: Quit, give up and go home.

*Champions do not become champions when
they win the event, but in the hours, weeks,
months and years they spend preparing for
it. The victorious performance itself is merely
the demonstration of their championship
character.* (T. Alan Armstrong)

On the other side, we have the "cloud of witnesses". Who are they? These in the grandstand are not "spectators" or "critics." NO, these are the ones who have finished the race of life. " They have done something with their lives and now sit in the places of honor. I call them the "unseen cloud of encouragers." You may not see them, but they are there cheering you on. You can be sure, for every set back, every failure, and yes even every success, someone up there has been through it before you. One of the greatest tricks that can be played on your mind is to convince you that no one knows how you feel, because this has never happened to anyone before. But, that's not true. It has before, and it will happen again.

He is not referring to the large number of people who occupy our pews who have veered off course and decided to "sit this one out." It's easy to sit in the grandstand at a football game on Saturday and tell the coach what to do. It's another thing to put on a uniform and get down on the field and fight for your team to win. The ones on the field don't have time to criticize the coach, the colors of the uniform or what the players next to them are doing wrong.

> **A critic is a legless man who teaches running.**
> **(Channing Pollack)**

THE ATTENTION WE MUST GIVE

"Let us throw off everything that hinders(weight) and the sin that so easily entangles,"

A Quick Analysis of the Race.

Life is not a game but a battle. It's hard fought. It's a tough minded race.

The word "race" is the Greek work *agona*. This is where we get the word "agony". Here is the picture of athletes in an agonizing footrace, running for the finish line, cheered on by the faithful Heros of past generations.

If we are going to be victorious in this arena, we must know there will be pain, heartache, sickness, sorrow, pressure and hardship, and even death. It's in this arena that our steel is tested. There is always going to be resistance to anything new. Whether it's a new idea for a business, or anything that upsets the "status quo," there will be those who will do everything they can to stop it.

> "Commitment is the enemy of resistance, for it is the serious promise to press on, to get up, no matter how many times you are knocked down." (David McNally)

The Preparation for the Race.

"Lay aside the weight." He's not just talking about sin. This could be "good" things not "bad" things.

We need "wings" not "weights." "Encumbrance" means excess weight, "mass" or "bulk." For a runner, it could be bulky sweat pants or leg weights. Can you imagine trying to run a race with your sweat pants on and two pound leg weights around your ankles? Every smart runner knows that he will never win a race like that.

For the Dreamer, it's anything that slows us down.

■ **Indifferent Attitude**

- **Mental Fatigue**
- **Procrastination**
- **Anything that Cuts into your Spiritual Passion**

Like a bad wardrobe of things we used to wear. We need to box them up and throw them away.

> **We are to take off the weights, but we must confess our unbelief**

"And sin" - What is the sin? In the context of Hebrews 10:12- I feel it's the sin of unbelief: "Which so easily ensnares us" or "besets us"? One word in the Greek text describes a "garment" that is wrapped around one's body and tied. It's used to describe a vine that climbs a tree and wraps around the trunk. We cannot run with sin wrapped around us.

The sin of unbelief to the Christian is like a "leg cramp" to the runner. If you have ever had a leg cramp you know how painful it can be. When a runner gets one, it can cause him to "hobble" off the track and put him on the sidelines. Today, we have many who for whatever reason, have taken themselves out of the race of life because something has wrapped around their legs and stopped them from "running."

THE ACTIVITY WE MUST EMPLOY

"and let us run with perseverance the race marked out for us."

Consider a few things about Running - First the Natural, Then the Spiritual.

- **Running Keeps You in Shape**

    Everyone who competes in the games goes

*into strict training. They do it to get a crown
that will not last; but we do it to get a crown
that will last forever. Therefore I do not run
like a man running aimlessly; I do not fight
like a man beating the air. No, I beat my
body and make it my slave so that after I
have preached to others, I myself will not be
disqualified for the prize.* (1 Cor 9:25-27)

*"If you have run with the footmen, and they
have wearied you, then how can you contend
with horses? And if in the land of peace, in
which you trusted, they wearied you, then
how will you do in the floodplain of the
Jordan?* (Jer 12:5)

Running in the natural helps to expend energy. You get energy
when you give energy. Same is true in the Spirit. There are too many
out of shape and lazy people.

■ **Running Keeps You Focused on the Goal**

*I press toward the mark for the prize of the
high calling of God in Christ Jesus.* (Phil 3:14)

We have all heard that old saying, "If you don't know where you
are going you could wind up someplace else." What are your goals for
the next 525,600 minutes? Don't be like the boy who shoots an arrow
at the barn and then paints a bull's-eye around it and says, "Look, I hit
the target!"

- **Running will help you get to where you want to go — just FASTER.**

There is a time to slow down and make sure you're going in the right direction. You never want to be like the man who tells his wife they are lost, but "we sure are making good time." Once you find your path to the goal, and you know this it's the direction you are to go in, then move ahead at full speed. Even race car drivers know that no matter how fast they are racing to the finish line, they have to check their mirrors, listen to the pit and watch those on either side. At the same time, they must keep their eyes on the checkered flag.

- **You Always Run Toward Something —Not Away from Something.**

What do you call someone who is running away from something, a thief or a coward?

A friend of mine told me a story of his son that fits here. He said, "I remember when my son was very small and he announced to me one day that he found a better way of walking. He called to me from the driveway and said, "Look dad, watch what I can do." I watched him as he started walking toward me BACKWARDS. It didn't take long before he bumped into the basketball goal and fell down. I laughed hard and said, "Son, that's good, but you can't go through the rest of your life walking backwards." A funny story, but the truth is, most of us spend too much time walking backwards through life.

- **Running toward a Goal you can See — Will Enable God to Move You Strategically Toward Goals You Can't See.**

It's called walking in the light you already have. Some people are always waiting for the lightning bolt to strike them and tell them the next move to make. While you're waiting for the next big revelation, why don't you keep moving forward with what you already know to do? We make it far more complicated than it really is. How do you know? The next email, the next phone call, the next letter in the mail or the next time you share the dream may be the one that will change your whole life.

THE ATTITUDE THAT SUSTAINS US

> Let us *fix our eyes on Jesus*, the author and perfecter of our faith, who for the joy set before him endured the cross, scorning its shame, and sat down at the right hand of the throne of God. **Consider** him who endured such opposition from sinful men, so that you will not grow weary and lose heart. (Heb 12:2-3)

Two important words here:

Endurance—or patience—or persistent perseverance

Runners call it "hitting the wall" or "second wind." It's when everything inside you is telling you to quit, but you break through. Every runner knows there is a critical time in the race when everything inside of you is screaming "GIVE UP!"

The ones who win are the ones who know how to push through the pain and never take their eyes off the finish line. Why would a runner get up before dawn, run hundreds of miles a week, endure hardship and bad weather, aching muscles and joints, and yet keep going? They know at the end of the day, in order to win the prize, they must endure to the end.

The Greek word for Endurance is described this way:

"The word is "hupomone" which does

not mean the patience which sits down
and accepts things but the patience which
masters them. It is not some romantic
thing which lends us wings to fly over
the difficulties and the hard places. It
is a determination, unhurrying and yet
undelaying, which goes steadily on and
refuses to be deflected. Obstacles do not
daunt it and discouragements do not take
its hope away. It is the steadfast endurance
which carries on until in the end it gets
there. "

They Sent Me To Finish

The Olympic Games, Mexico, 1968. The marathon is the final event on the program. The Olympic stadium is packed, and there is excitement as the first athlete, an Ethiopian runner, enters the stadium. The crowd erupts as he crosses the finish line.

Way back in the field is another runner, John Stephen Akwhari of Tanzania. He has been eclipsed by the other runners. After 30 kilometers his head is throbbing, his muscles are aching and he falls to the ground. He has serious leg injuries and officials want him to retire, but he refuses. With his knee bandaged, Akwhari picks himself up and hobbles the remaining 12 kilometers to the finish line. An hour after the winner has finished Akwhari enters the stadium. All but a few thousand of the crowd have gone home. Akwhari moves around the track at a painstakingly slow pace, until finally he collapses over the finish line.

It is one of the most heroic efforts of Olympic history. Afterward, asked by a reporter why he had not dropped out, Akwhari says, "My country did not send me 10,000 miles just to start the race; they sent me to finish the race." From Wikipedia

Encouragement—"Fixing our Eyes On Jesus"— "Consider Him" Fixing our Eyes means - "aphorao" - To look away from all else and fix one's gaze upon." Not only at the first moment of the race, but constantly during the whole struggle. As runners, our eyes must be on him, not looking to see where the other runners are, nor listening to the crowd.

> The Greeks had a race in their Olympic games that was unique. The winner was not the runner who finished first. It was the runner who finished with his torch still lit. I want to run all the way with the flame of my torch still lit for Him. (J. Stowell Moody, Fan The Flame)

Consider Him — To reckon, compare, weigh, think over. The point is to develop such a positive mental attitude that it will allow us to hang tough and fight off mental fatigue and frustration.

> Deciding to take up jogging, the man was astounded by the wide selection of jogging shoes available at the local sports shoe store. While trying on a basic pair of jogging shoe, he noticed a minor feature and asked the clerk: "What is this little pocket thing here on the side for?" And the clerk: "Oh, that's to carry spare change so you can call your wife to come pick you up when you've jogged too far."

How?

■ **Claim the Grace to Persevere.**

When all are against you and your legs give way, when you're out of breath and strength, call on God for the second wind; The Grace to go on. The will of God will never take you where the grace of God can't keep you. God's grace and his strength will support and sustain you in the race of life.

■ **Remember You Are Not Alone.**

The feeling of being alone has caused more people to get off the track or just give up. Remember, our strength will be renewed when we know generations of faithful believers have gone before us.

It's time to make up your mind. What will you do with the time you have left? Will you look back over your life and grieve over wasted years, or will you decide today to do something about the opportunities that are right before you?

You've been promising yourself for too long that you're going to get in the race and run. Time to quit talking and time to start running your race!

CHAPTER 11

Finding Your Purpose
Everyone Has One

This is not to assume that you are not living out your purpose. But, it is surprising how many people get up every day without knowing why they are alive. They go to work, come home, do chores and live their lives in quiet desperation. It doesn't have to be this way. As a matter of fact, you can determine today to change things. It's all a matter of choice. You can decide that today things are going to be different.

Ask yourself the following questions:

■ **What is my burden?**

> *"I speak the truth in Christ—I am not lying, my conscience confirms it through the Holy Spirit— 2 I have great sorrow and unceasing anguish in my heart. 3 For I could wish that I myself were cursed and cut off from Christ for the sake of my people, those of my own race."*
> (Romans 9:1-3)

What do you feel strongly about? When talking to someone, what is the one thing that you can't stop talking about? Is it starting a new business, a new ministry or becoming a better parent? Burden can only come when you allow yourself to be touched by someone or by something.

When the enemy attacks, it's your burden that will keep you

moving, or you will give up.

Whatever it is, take time and write it down and keep it in front of you every day.

■ What is my vision?

> *"Where there is no revelation, people cast off restraint; but blessed is the one who heeds wisdom's instruction."* (Proverbs 29:18)

What do see yourself doing about your burden? A vision without a burden makes you someone who talks a good game but does nothing about it. A burden without a vision will make you task oriented, and you will eventually burn out. A vision attached to a burden will move you forward to success.

Don't let the feeling of inadequacy stop you from pursuing your vision. God took Moses, who had nothing but a burden for his people, and gave him a vision to set them free. If he can take a man (Moses) with just a stick and a stammer, just think what He can do for you.

■ What is my strategy?

> *Then the LORD replied:"Write down the revelation and make it plain on tablets so that a herald may run with it. For the revelation awaits an appointed time; it speaks of the end and will not prove false. Though it linger, wait for it; it will certainly come and will not delay."* (Habakkuk 2:2-3)

What plans do you have to realize your burden/vision? What

about training, study or finances? What opportunities exist that you can take advantage of? What immediate steps in pursuing your vision can you take today?

A vision without a plan is just wishful thinking. A strategy is an action plan to get your vision from your mind to your feet.

Four Types of Strategy

1. ### THE "TRADITIONAL" APPROACH.
    We have been doing the same thing for the last 50 years. It was good enough for grandma, and it's good enough for me. We are happy to report that we have been against every move of God for the past two generations.

2. ### THE "DON'T PLAN" APPROACH.
    Just let the Holy Spirit come, and He will do everything. Just sit back and do nothing. We are too spiritual to get our hands dirty and work toward our vision.

3. ### THE "START BUT DON'T FINISH" APPROACH.
    It's called the "Big Bang" theory. Start it, make a lot of noise, get people excited, and then lose interest and let people wonder "what happened."

4. ### THE "UNIQUE PLAN" APPROACH.
    What is God saying to us now? Do we need to stop what we're doing and try a new approach? Most businesses and churches that go under never try the one approach that might work. If what you are doing is not working, maybe it's time to try something different.

WHAT ARE MY RESOURCES?

Who are "resource" people that have the maturity and experience you can call on for advice? There are people all around you that can be a great help and resource to you. For the most part, you are one person removed from the open door you need for success.

Find someone who has already "been there, done that," and find out what they did to achieve their success. Read all their books. Listen to their tapes. Go to their seminars. If possible, interview them. Don't reinvent the wheel. Learn from those who have a proven track record of success.

> **If you're not planning to succeed,
> you are planning for failure**

All of us need at least three resource relationships in our life:

Paul: Someone who has gone before us. He will alert us to watch out for potholes and ditches.

Timothy: Someone who will come behind us. Having a Timothy keeps you sharp. It's exciting to watch our Timothy's grow and mature.

Barnabas: Someone who will stand shoulder to shoulder with us: A peer level relationship. Barnabas will speak truth, in love, to us.

Three Golden Keys

1. SOW POSITIVE INFLUENCE SEEDS

I have taught many times that you only reap what you sow. Seed sowing is a law of nature and a spiritual law, as well. What God did in the natural, He has a correlation in the spiritual realm. You can't reap a harvest, if you haven't planted any seed. There is no such thing as spontaneous generation. Nothing comes into existence in and of itself. If you want be successful, sow success seeds in someone else. What you make happen for others God will make happen for you. Remember, what you seed is what you get. I am convinced that you can seed your way to success.

There is a big difference between a farmer who "wants" a harvest and one who "expects" a harvest. He can want a harvest, work hard, get up early and do all the right things and still go hungry. Why? He must do the most important thing, and that is sow seed in the ground. Once the seed is planted, he can now say he not only wants a harvest, but he's expecting one. Seed time and harvest is a God ordained principle in the natural world and in the spiritual world.

It's a fact you are a:

- **Conduit of Blessings to Others**
- **Store House of Seed Waiting to be Released**
- **A person of Influence and Favor**
- **The Apple of God's Eye**

> *If you can dream it, then you can achieve it.*
> *You will get all you want in life if you help*
> *enough other people get what they want.* (Zig Ziglar)

2.   RELEASE WHAT'S IN YOUR HAND

There is a principle that says, "When you release what's in your hand, God will release what's in His hand."   If you keep what's in your hand, it can only do what you can do. When you release what's in your hand to God, then it can do what He can do. You would have to agree, He can do "exceedingly, abundantly above all that we ask or think, according to the power that works in us." Ephesians 3:20

There may be times when we know we should "seed" for success, but our mind tells us to "hold on" to what we have. The world system has convinced us that there is "shortage" everywhere, and if we let go, there won't be anymore. That's a lie! The greatest leader/teacher who ever lived said it best, "Give and it will be given to you, good measure, pressed down, shaken together, and running over will be put into your bosom. For with the same measure that you use, it will be measured back to you". Luke 6:38

What Seed Can You Release Today?

- Words of Encouragement
- Financial Blessings
- Time
- Showing Favor to Someone
- Love
- Friendliness
- Mercy

And so much more!

> "You must give some time to your fellow men. Even if it's a little thing, do something for others - something for which you get no pay but the privilege of doing it." (Albert Schweitzer)

> "Blessed are those who can give without remembering and take without forgetting." (Elizabeth Bibesco)

> "Let me do all the good I can, to all the people I can, as often as I can, for I shall not pass this way again." (John Wesley)

3. Don't Look Back

Many people define their life by their failures, not their successes. All your life experiences have been designed by God to use for your growth and maturity. Most of the people I've met over the last thirty five years (if they are honest with me) feel poorly about themselves. At some point, most of us have experienced failure and disappointment. The sad truth is many people organize their life around some experience that left them with the accusation of the devil that they will never be useful again.

It may be something that happened before they met Christ or after they became a child of God, either way, it stays with them. They are constantly looking over their shoulder. When some new venture is attempted and criticism comes, invariably they will revert back to a past failure and stop short of success. Blame sets in, and they are pulled into the dark hole of despair.

Stand up to the twin killers of hope and encouragement.

- First, **guilt** which speaks of **wickedness**
Guilt says, I made a mistake, and I can never recover.
- Second, **shame** which speaks of **worthlessness**
Shame says, I am a mistake, and God will never use me.

But, here's the good news. You are not a mistake. When God created you He knew exactly what He was doing. He didn't look at you and say, "Well I really messed up this time!" NO! You are God's workmanship; a prized possession. He will never define your life by your mistakes, so why do you?

God told Jeremiah

> "Before I formed you in the womb I knew
> you; before you were born I sanctified you;
> I ordained you a prophet to the nations."
> (Jeremiah 1:5)

John the Baptist was called by God before his birth

> "For he (John) will be great in the sight of
> the Lord, and shall drink neither wine, nor
> strong drink. He will also be filled with the
> Holy Spirit, even from his mother's womb."
> (John 1:15)

Paul, the great apostle, knew that God had a plan for his life

> "But when it pleased God, who separated
> me from my mother's womb and called me
> through His grace, to reveal His Son in me,
> that I might preach Him among the Gentiles,
> I did not immediately confer with flesh and
> blood." (Galatians 1:15-16)

- Jeremiah wanted to quit — but pushed through to become a great prophet
- John the Baptist was put in jail and was filled with doubt, yet Jesus said no man born of woman was greater
- Paul was a persecutor of the Church and yet wrote three fourths of the New Testament.

"Many of life's failures are people who did
not realize how close they were to success
when they gave up" (Thomas A Edison)

Everyone makes mistakes. Even men and women of the Bible
and human history made mistakes and failed. However, many of them
used their failures as "stepping stones" not "tombstones."

You can live a life of victory in spite of criticism, past failures and
disappointments. You have in you the power to live an overcoming
life.

Every time the enemy tries to talk about your past just remind
him what the Lord has done for you. You are forgiven, redeemed, and
favored child of God. Remind him that you have royal blood flowing
in your veins, and as a "Kings" kid, you have the power to live a life
of victory.

*Greater is He that is in you than he that is in
the world."* (1 John 4:4)

'I have missed more than 9,000 shots in
my career. I have lost almost 300 games.
On 26 occasions I have been entrusted
to take the game winning shot… and I
missed. I have failed over and over and over
again in my life. And that's precisely why I
succeed." (Michael Jordan)

CHAPTER 12

When That Which You Love Has Died
Time to Raise the Dead

In the natural world, the minute something is given life, it begins to die. We generally don't like to think of life in these terms, but it's the truth. The aging process is a natural thing. It begins at birth and ends with death. Bound by time, everything and everyone will eventually die physically, save those who are alive at the coming of the Lord, and even they will see their earthly bodies no more. And life is like that roll of toilet paper: The closer you get to the end the faster it goes.

In the spiritual realm, God has ordained a way for us to live forever, but guess what? It involves dying. Everything around us and everything in us operates within the immutable laws of creation and the present will of God. He has "appointed unto man" a time to die and a time to be raised again. (Hebrews 9:27) The writer of Ecclesiastes said, "That everything has its place in time, including birth and death."

Each of us, believers and non-believers alike, grieve when something or someone we love dies. We grieve because we have been diminished by the death of that which was a part of our own lives. We grieve because, at some level, we realize that with every death we observe, we are reminded of our own mortality.

Whether we become philosophical in regard to death, or rail at the devil or even God, the fact remains: things die. It is a most sobering and sorrowful occasion, however, to be witness to the death of a vision or dream, especially if it happens to be our own. We know that God through Jesus has won the victory over death, hell and the grave. Why is it we have a difficult time applying this victory to our vision and destiny? God is able to raise up dreams, visions and ministries that, for whatever reason, have died. He is able to restore to the fullest.

> *"And I will restore to you the years that the*
> *locust hath eaten, the cankerworm, and the*
> *caterpillar, and the palmerworm, my great*
> *army which I sent among you. And ye shall*
> *eat in plenty, and be satisfied, and praise the*
> *name of the LORD your God, that hath dealt*
> *wondrously with you: and my people shall*
> *never be ashamed. And ye shall know that*
> *I am in the midst of Israel, and that I am*
> *the LORD your God, and none else: and my*
> *people shall never be ashamed." (Joel 2:25-27)*

And friend, God doesn't just start us over, he makes up for those lost years and opportunities. What do we do when vision dies, and we aren't even sure how it happened? We just woke up one day and it was gone. We can blame our family or our friends. We can blame the church, the pastor, our upline, but it won't bring back the dead. It's gone.

The Lazarus Principle

Jesus was traveling through the region in which John the Baptist first began to proclaim the coming of the Lord when the word came of Lazarus' sickness. Not just anyone, but one "Whom you love is sick." Jesus makes a very bold statement. *"This sickness is not unto death, but for the glory of God."* Interesting, isn't it? Jesus knew before hand that, by the time He got to Bethany, Lazarus would be in a tomb.

They don't usually put you there unless you are dead. In fact, by the time Jesus arrived, Lazarus was not only dead - he was stinking dead! More on that later . . . .

The Difference Between Facts and Truth

The facts said one thing, but the Lord said another. In their grief, Lazarus family and friends could not see beyond the facts to know that the Truth was standing among them! Let's contrast fact and truth:

Fact: **Lazarus is dying . . . and now he is dead.**
Truth: **The giver of life is on the way
and has already spoken words of Truth.**

Fact: **Lazarus is in the grave and has been there long
enough to begin to decay.**
Truth: **The One who has come to defeat death
is beginning to speak.**

Fact: **Lazarus is standing at the entrance to the sepulcher!**
Truth: **Jesus isn't through, yet. He commands them to
remove the grave clothes.**

Fact: **Your dreams may look as dead as four o'clock!**
Truth: **The One who first gave them can
indeed resurrect them!**

If we believe what the facts tell us, we may miss the Truth of God. If we believe the Truth, the facts will eventually line up. God gave you that dream and destiny, and God can speak life into it again.

DEFINING VISION

Proverbs 29:18 says, *"Where there is no vision* (prophetic revelation), *the people perish* (cast off restraint)." When a leader has no fresh revelation from the Word of God, he finds himself wandering in the wilderness without direction or motivation. Self-doubt, indecision and frustration become his constant companions. The people he is supposed to be leading become a mirror of his own deficiencies. Someone once asked Helen Keller if she knew of anything worse than being blind. "Yes," she said; "It's someone who can see, but who has no vision." Habakkuk 2:2 records, *"Write the vision and make it plain upon the tablets, that he may run who reads it."*

There is supernatural power in a God-given vision. There is *creative* power to accomplish something that has never been done. There is the power of *commitment* beyond our human capacity to be faithful. There is the power of *contagion* when "deep calls unto deep" and the Spirit bears witness of the voice of the Lord. There is the power to *change* ordinary individuals into a mighty army which will rout the enemy at every turn. There is the power of leaving behind a *continuing* legacy which will serve future generations, and upon which those generations can build *their* dreams.

With all this miraculous power available, it seems contradictory to even suggest that any vision might one day cease to be, but the truth is evident, even visions die. Let us remember, though, that everything we call dead may not be dead in God's eyes.

The Reason Death Comes
(first the natural, then the spiritual)

■ **The Natural Aging Process:** In the natural, as we have said, things get older and don't work as well as before. Our bodies, under the curse, will sooner or later weaken to the point that they can no longer support life. In the Spirit, we "age" when we have finished those things we were created to do. I don't want to die "full," with things left undone regarding purpose. I want to die "empty," having accomplished all that He put in my hands to achieve. Jesus, hanging on the cross, was able to say, "It is finished." Paul, writing in 2 Timothy 4:6-7, exclaims, *"For I am now ready to be offered, and the time of my departure is at hand. I have fought a good fight, I have finished my course, I have kept the faith."*

■ **Murder:** In this present evil world, people kill people every day. It has become so common and so commonly reported that only the most heinous and terrible killings receive more than a passing interest. The fact that the Enemy still has a measure of power on the earth is evidenced daily in every form of news media. Abortion is murder of the highest order. Satan is a destroyer, and he *is* destroying. Spiritual abortions take place every day as well. Revelation 12:1-4 is a picture of the desire of the Enemy to abort the purpose of God. He will abort ours, as well, if we aren't on our guard.

> *"And there appeared a great wonder in heaven; a woman clothed with the sun, and the moon under her feet, and upon her head a crown of twelve stars: And she being with child cried, travailing in birth, and pained to be delivered. And there appeared another wonder in heaven; and behold a great red dragon, having seven heads and ten horns, and seven crowns upon his heads. And his tail drew the third part of the stars of heaven, and did cast them to the earth: and the dragon stood before the woman which was*

ready to be delivered, for to devour her child
as soon as it was born." (Revelation 12:1-4)

■ **Suicide:** As precious as life is to most of us, there are
unfortunately too many who have fallen so deeply into despair
that they are convinced that life is not worth living, and that the
lives of those around them would be better served without them.
Hardly a family has escaped the tragedy of losing a loved one to
their own hand. Ministers and pastors aren't exempt, either. The
writer of Proverbs tells us that *"Hope deferred maketh the heart*
sick." Spiritual suicide is probably even more common than physical
suicide. The pressures of the expectations of life, self-imposed
drives to be supermen and women, and constantly operating outside
our anointing and gifting can lead to a sense of hopelessness and
despair. Spiritual self-destruction results, not in physical death, but
in unfulfilled dreams and leads to the execution of our calling by our
own confused, desperate hand.

■ **Disease:** New illnesses, viruses and cell-destroying micro-
organisms are being identified and reported almost daily.
Researchers and technicians work around the clock to develop
effective weapons and cures. The most insidious of all is the
disease that weakens the body's ability to fight disease - AIDS. In
the spirit realm, the Enemy sees to it that the seeds of spiritual
sickness are sown into every vision and dream. In order to fight, our
supernatural immune system must be in top condition at all times.
Anything that can weaken, debilitate or cripple our vision must be
attacked with the "antibodies" of the Word of God! Paul's prayer for
the church was, *"That he would grant you, according to the riches of*
his glory, to be strengthened with might by his Spirit in the inner man."
(Ephesians 3:16)

■   **Accident:** In the natural, these deaths are the hardest to deal with. Why does a child die? Why is one taken in the prime years of life? Why does the drunk driver live and the young family go? We call them accidents, because they are out of the natural order of birth, life and death. "Spiritual accidents" almost seems like an oxymoron. They do occur, however, in the sense that our dreams and goals can slip from our grasp seemingly overnight. The truth is, that it usually takes more than one blow to our blind side to end our destiny. These kinds of "accidents" are the result of built up resentment, frustration and anger which finally explode - and we do something foolish. The key to avoiding this kind of death is to deal with each circumstance quickly and completely, never allowing them to feed off each other and grow. Accidents are the leading cause of death - physically and in the spirit.

FOUR PRINCIPLES FOR RAISING DEAD VISION

■   **The Dead Friend Principle**
Is the death of vision final? Remember, Jesus looks at death from a different perspective. In the story of Lazarus, He first told His disciples Lazarus was *sleeping*. (John 11) When they misunderstood Him to mean resting, only then did Jesus use the word *dead*. Did Lazarus respond to the voice of the Lord and walk out of the grave? Can the One who called him from the grip of death speak to your "sleeping" vision? "But Lord, my dream has been dead for some time. Surely by now it smells. If only you had been here when it was clinging to life. I know you could have 'healed' it. Why didn't you come sooner?" Tell me, from which does God receive greater glory; healing the sick, or raising to life that which has died? Beyond that, while our dream lived, did we not claim a certain amount of ownership and credit? When it died, we disowned it, which is what God was after in the first

place. Now we are convinced of His ownership - and our stewardship. I call it the "Dead Friend" principle. The lesson of Lazarus is that delay does not mean defeat! It may look and even smell dead, but at the Word of the Lord it will stand and live again! They thought as long as there was life there's hope. But God is reminding us that as long as there is Jesus there is hope. Jesus trumps and triumphs over all things dead.

■ The Dead Son Principle

The second principle of reviving vision is what I call the "Dead Son" principle. Remember the story of the Prophet Elisha and the barren Shunammite woman in 2 Kings 4? She had no child, and because of her kindness to him, Elisha got a word from the Lord that she would bear a son.

> "And he said, About this season, according to the time of life, thou shalt embrace a son. And she said, Nay, my lord, thou man of God, do not lie unto thine handmaid. And the woman conceived, and bare a son at that season that Elisha had said unto her, according to the time of life." (2 Kings 4:16-17)

The child grew, and when he was able, went out into the field to work with his father. Suddenly, falling down ill (probably from heat stroke), he was carried to his mother's lap where he died. (2 Kings 4:20) Doing the only thing she knew to do, the woman went immediately to see Elisha and brought him back to her house. Elisha prayed and the Lord answered his prayer. The child sneezed seven times and got up!

The promises God has given us may seem to have died prematurely. We may even be asking why God would allow us to have hope and then take it away. We may not understand everything that happens, but we can know with perfect assurance that, *"He which hath begun a good work in you will perform it until the day of Jesus Christ."* (Philippians 1:6) If God has promised that you will "give birth" to your vision, believe it. Though it may appear to be dead, let the Shunammite's words echo from your lips: *"'Is it well with the child?' And she answered, 'It is well.'"* (2 Kings 4:26) A prophetic word given is a prophetic word fulfilled. God does what He says He will do!

■ The Dead Womb Principle

The third principle for reviving vision is the "Dead Womb" principle. Look at Luke 1:7-13:

> *"And they had no child, because that Elisabeth was barren, and they both were now well stricken in years. And it came to pass, that while he executed the priest's office before God in the order of his course, according to the custom of the priest's office, his lot was to burn incense when he went into the temple of the Lord. And the whole multitude of the people were praying without at the time of incense. And there appeared unto him an angel of the Lord standing on the right side of the altar of incense. And when Zacharias saw him, he was troubled, and fear fell upon him. But the angel said unto him, Fear not, Zacharias: for thy prayer is heard; and thy wife Elisabeth shall bear thee a son, and thou shalt call his name John."*

The truth of this passage is to always depend upon what God has said and not go by what has or hasn't happened. Don't look at the passing of time, look to God's *timing*. Many people who have heard God speak concerning destiny become discouraged when it seems that too much time has passed. The scripture records that Zacharias and Elizabeth were "well stricken" (well along) in years. No doubt they had prayed for many years for an heir to carry the family name. No doubt, as well, that they had long since failed to believe it would happen. God doesn't own a calendar, and He doesn't look at time or age. He didn't need a John the Baptist years earlier when Zacharias and Elizabeth were praying for a son. He needed him now, when it was time to prepare the way for Jesus. God had ordained that Elizabeth's son would arrive when it was time to announce to the world that *His* son was on the way! I don't know about you, but I want the birth of my vision to be absolutely in time with what God is doing through His son!

■ The Dead Business or Ministry Principle

The fourth principle is the principle of the "Dead Business (ministry)." The subtitle for this section could be, "Failure is only temporary." In Exodus chapters three and four, we have the record of the Lord's appearance to Moses in the burning bush. We need to back up, though, to a day in Egypt years before Moses tried to liberate his people by taking on their captors one at a time. Because he was doing things his way and not God's, he failed miserably. Forty years of self-imposed exile, leading sheep instead of a nation, had taken it's toll. His objections to the Lord's call reveal his sense of personal failure. (refer to chapter five, *Mapping Your Destiny*)

God's answer to Moses' objections was to turn the very symbol of his failure (the shepherd's rod) into a sign of His power. What had been *a* rod, became *the* rod, and finally the *rod of God*. What had been a tool in the hand of a man was now a weapon of deliverance in the hand of the Lord! What, to you, symbolizes the failure or death of your dreams? A business? A broken home? Financial failure? It is the heart of God to turn the very thing that haunts you into an instrument of His glory. Failure is not fatal, nor is it final. What it is, or can be, is a learning experience upon which we rebuild a stronger foundation for vision.

Do you remember the excitement and zeal of those first few years of walking in the calling of God? Do you yearn for that fervor and intensity? Turn aside to your "burning bush," and allow Him to change your failure into fruitfulness. Recapture and revive your vision by:

Going back to where you left it. Returning to your first love. Stand again on the Word you received. It's as true as it ever was! Confessing the promises of God. They are "yea and amen!" Taking responsibility for your current situation. Blaming others will always provide the excuse you need to remain in the desert.

Dear brothers and sisters, we are privileged to be living in the most exciting time of God's plan and purpose in the history of the world. We have not even begun to see or even sense the magnificent things He intends to do in this generation and those to follow. As we have said, He is moving, and He is quickening the pace. With all the desire of my heart, I want you to hear me: God's heart and His will is to use *you* to accomplish great things in His Kingdom's work. Henry T. Blackerby says in *Experiencing God*, "God's will is not something He *wants* to do - it is something He is *now doing*. He's inviting us to come along with Him, and I'm anticipating a great journey! Won't you come, too?

*"Eye hath not seen, nor ear heard, neither
have entered into the heart of man, the things
which God hath prepared for them that love
him. But God hath revealed them unto us by
his Spirit: for the Spirit searcheth all things,
yea, the deep things of God."* (1 Corinthians
2:9-10)

Re-Establishing Leadership
(8 LAWS FOR LEADING)

1. ### THE LAW OF DECISION MAKING
   People follow the leader who decides well when questions arise as the group moves toward accomplishing their objective. So decide to lead and become a doer and not just a hearer.

2. ### THE LAW OF DREAMS
   People follow a leader who has a dream of a desirable objective. When people buy into a leader's dreams, they buy into his/her leadership.

3. ### THE LAW OF REWARDS
   People follow a leader who rewards them when they accomplish their goals, which ensures they will continue to follow him.

4. ### THE LAW OF CREDIBILITY
   People follow a leader when they have confidence in his plans. The leader who believes in his followers usually has people who believe in him.

5. ### THE LAW OF MOTIVATION
   People follow a leader who effectively communicates his plan

to reach the objective. People tend to follow a leader who gives clear directions.

6. **THE LAW OF ACCOUNTABILITY**
The leader must give specific responsibilities and know the specific contribution his followers can make to help ensure the entire group reaches the goal. Then he must hold each group member accountable to do his part.

7. **THE LAW OF COMMUNICATION**
Motivation is not stirring speeches, slogans or threats. People tend to follow a leader who gives them compelling reasons to do so. People follow you when you give them a reason to work.

8. **THE LAW OF PROBLEM SOLVING**
People follow a leader who gives solutions to problems that hinder them from reaching the objective. The more barriers that frustrate your followers, the less likely your followers are to reach their goal.

Come on in to the "deep end" of the things of the Spirit. The water's fine!

CHAPTER 13

Daily Confession
Release Your Full Potential Daily

This is the day God has designed for me. Throughout this day, I will move closer to my destiny. Because I was created on purpose, I will live this day with purpose.

AND SO I PURPOSE TODAY TO:
- Choose life and not death.
- Choose love and not hate.
- Choose faith and not doubt.
- Choose kindness and not unkindness.
- Choose forgiveness and not unforgiveness
- Choose peace and not frustration.
- Choose patience and not turmoil.
- Choose right and not wrong.
- Choose to move on and not stay the same.

THIS IS MY DAY TO:
- Learn something new.
- Meet somebody different.
- Look for someone to show the plan to.
- Find some way to share the dream.
- Realize my some day is today.

TODAY I WILL:

- Treasure my family by loving them.
- Honor my leaders by following them.
- Respect my mentors by listening to them.
- Please my God by obeying Him.

THIS IS MY DAY TO SUCCEED, TRIUMPH, OVERCOME, AND BE VICTORIOUS. I WILL MEET:

- Every challenge with faith.
- Every opposition with courage.
- Every struggle with resolve.

Because, I know that I'm on the right side, joined to the right team, with the right people, excited about the right mission, for the right reason.

This day is my day, my opportunity, and my time to move on—by God's grace. Today, not tomorrow—I will move one step closer to my destiny by RELEASING MY FULL POTENTIAL.

UNBELIEF SAYS:
Some other year—but not this year
Some other business—but not my business
Some other person—but not through me

I REPENT OF THE SIN OF UNBELIEF AND BELIEVE BY FAITH:

That anything God did in any other year
He'll do this year
And anything God did in any other business
He'll do in my business

**And anything God did through any other person
He'll do through me.**

**SO DO IT LORD, THIS YEAR, IN MY BUSINESS
THROUGH ME, FOR YOUR GLORY AND YOUR
HONOR, AMEN.**

■ MINISTRY RESOURCES AND INFORMATION

PAUL E. TSIKA MINISTRIES INC
RESTORATION RANCH
P.O. BOX 136 (5351 HIGHWAY 71)
MIDFIELD, TEXAS 77458

WEB SITE: WWW.PLOWON.ORG
OFFICE PHONE: 361-588-7190
EMAIL: mark@plowon.org